CCDA/CCDP ~~Study~~

CCDA/CCDP Flash Cards and Exam Practice Pack

Anthony Sequeira

Kevin Wallace, CCIE No. 7945

Cisco Press

800 East 96th Street
Indianapolis, IN 46240 USA

CCDA/CCDP Flash Cards and Exam Practice Pack

Anthony Sequeira

Kevin Wallace

Copyright© 2004 Cisco Systems, Inc.

Published by:
Cisco Press
800 East 96th Street
Indianapolis, IN 46240 USA

Printed in the United States of America   1 2 3 4 5 6 7 8 9 0

Library of Congress Cataloging-in-Publication Number: 2003116491

ISBN: 1-58720-117-8

First Printing   February 2004

Trademark Acknowledgments

Warning and Disclaimer

Corporate and Government Sales

Cisco Press offers excellent discounts on this book when ordered in quantity for bulk purchases or special sales.

For more information, please contact: **U.S. Corporate and Government Sales** 1-800-382-3419 corpsales@pearsontechgroup.com

For sales outside of the U.S. please contact: **International Sales** 1-317-581-3793 international@pearsontechgroup.com

Feedback Information

At Cisco Press, our goal is to create in-depth technical books of the highest quality and value. Each book is crafted with care and precision, undergoing rigorous development that involves the unique expertise of members from the professional technical community.

Readers' feedback is a natural continuation of this process. If you have any comments regarding how we could improve the quality of this book, or otherwise alter it to better suit your needs, you can contact us through e-mail at feedback@ciscopress.com. Please make sure to include the book title and ISBN in your message.

We greatly appreciate your assistance.

Publisher	John Wait
Editor-in-Chief	John Kane
Executive Editor	Brett Bartow
Acquisitions Editor	Michelle Grandin
Cisco Representative	Anthony Wolfenden
Cisco Press Program Manager	Nannette M. Noble
Production Manager	Patrick Kanouse
Senior Editor	Sheri Cain
Copy Editor	Bridget Collins
Technical Editors	Andy Barkl, Matt Birkner, Jesse J. Herrera
Media Developers	Brandon Penticuff, Boson Software
Team Coordinator	Tammi Barnett
Cover Designer	Louisa Adair
Composition	Mark Shirar
Proofreader	Angela Rosio

CISCO SYSTEMS

Corporate Headquarters	European Headquarters	Americas Headquarters	Asia Pacific Headquarters
Cisco Systems, Inc.	Cisco Systems International BV	Cisco Systems, Inc.	Cisco Systems, Inc.
170 West Tasman Drive	Haarlerbergpark	170 West Tasman Drive	Capital Tower
San Jose, CA 95134-1706	Haarlerbergweg 13-19	San Jose, CA 95134-1706	168 Robinson Road
USA	1101 CH Amsterdam	USA	#22-01 to #29-01
www.cisco.com	The Netherlands	www.cisco.com	Singapore 068912
Tel: 408 526-4000	www.europe.cisco.com	Tel: 408 526-7660	www.cisco.com
800 553-NETS (6387)	Tel: 31 0 20 357 1000	Fax: 408 527-0883	Tel: +65 6317 7777
Fax: 408 526-4100	Fax: 31 0 20 357 1100		Fax: +65 6317 7799

Cisco Systems has more than 200 offices in the following countries and regions. Addresses, phone numbers, and fax numbers are listed on the
Cisco.com Web site at www.cisco.com/go/offices.

Argentina • Australia • Austria • Belgium • Brazil • Bulgaria • Canada • Chile • China PRC • Colombia • Costa Rica • Croatia • Czech Republic
Denmark • Dubai, UAE • Finland • France • Germany • Greece • Hong Kong SAR • Hungary • India • Indonesia • Ireland • Israel • Italy
Japan • Korea • Luxembourg • Malaysia • Mexico • The Netherlands • New Zealand • Norway • Peru • Philippines • Poland • Portugal
Puerto Rico • Romania • Russia • Saudi Arabia • Scotland • Singapore • Slovakia • Slovenia • South Africa • Spain • Sweden
Switzerland • Taiwan • Thailand • Turkey • Ukraine • United Kingdom • United States • Venezuela • Vietnam • Zimbabwe

About the Authors

Anthony Sequeira holds almost every major Microsoft and Cisco professional certification. For the past 10 years, he has written and lectured to massive audiences about the latest in networking technologies. Anthony is currently a senior technical instructor and certified Cisco Systems instructor for KnowledgeNet. He lives with his wife and daughter in Massachusetts and is an extremely passionate Red Sox fan despite "the curse."

Kevin Wallace, CCIE No. 7945, is a certified Cisco Systems instructor and a full-time instructor for KnowledgeNet, a pioneer of next-generation e-learning. With 14 years of Cisco networking experience, Kevin has been a network design specialist for the Walt Disney World Resort and a network manager for Eastern Kentucky University. He holds a bachelor of science in electrical engineering from the University of Kentucky. Kevin also holds the CCNP and CCDP certifications, and two IP Telephony specializations.

About the Technical Reviewers

Andy Barkl has more than 19 years of experience in the IT field. He is the owner of MCT & Associates, LLC, a technical training and consulting firm in Phoenix, Arizona. He enjoys dividing his time between classroom, writing, and consulting on Cisco and Windows deployments. He is also the online editor for MCPMag.com, TCPMag.com, CertCities.com, and a contributing author and editor for Cisco Press and Sybex. He hosts several monthly exam-preparation chats on MCPMag.com, TCPMag.com, and CertCities.com. Andy holds the following certifications: CCNP, CCDP, CISSP, MCT, MCSE: Security, MCSA: Security, MCSA: Messaging, A+, CTT+, i-Net+, Network+, Security+, Server+, and CNA.

Matthew H. Birkner, CCIE, is a network-consulting engineer who works for Cisco Systems in the Network Supported Accounts (NSA) Program. He currently supports and designs enterprise networks. Matt has been a network design engineer, network operations center engineer, and technical support specialist. He also holds the CCDP certification, and is a Certified Netware Engineer (CNE) and Bay Networks Certified Specialist (BNCS).

Jesse J. Herrera is a senior systems analyst for a Fortune 100 Company located in Houston, Texas. Jesse holds a bachelor of science in computer science from the University of Arizona and a master of science in telecommunications management from Southern Methodist University. His current Cisco certifications include CCNP and CCDP.

Dedications

Anthony Sequeira:

I would like to dedicate this book to my beautiful daughter, Annabella Joy Sequeira. You are the most incredible gift a man could receive.

Kevin Wallace:

I dedicate this book to my daughters, Sabrina and Stacie, who constantly remind me of the joy found in learning, and to my wife Vivian for her love, encouragement, and support along our way to forever together.

Acknowledgments

Anthony Sequeira:

As always, thanks to my wife Joette for her patience and understanding during my frequent weekend-writing projects!

Thanks to Tom Warrick, Frank Gartland, and all the other incredibly talented employees of KnowledgeNet. You have had such a profound effect on my career—it is amazing!

Thanks also to all the awesome people at Cisco Press—especially Brett Bartow and Michelle Grandin.

Kevin Wallace:

Thanks to my family for their inspiration and support. Viv, you are an amazing wife, and I love you with all of my heart. Stacie, I am so proud to be your Dad. Your kind heart and brilliant mind will lead you to success in whatever you do. Sabrina, I'm equally proud to be your Dad. Your infectious laughter, beautiful smile, and love for learning make you an all-around winner. Most of all, I thank my Heavenly Father, who directs my steps.

Thanks to Tom Warrick, Frank Gartland, and the entire KnowledgeNet team. You constantly encourage me to be the best I can be.

Another big thanks to my co-author, Anthony Sequeira. You gave me the opportunity to join you in this endeavor, and it has been an honor. Finally, thank you to Michelle Grandin at Cisco Press, who made the work on this book a pleasure.

Table of Contents

Foreword

CCDA/CCDP Flash Cards and Exam Practice Pack is a late-stage
practice tool that provides you with a variety of proven exam-
preparation methods, including physical and electronic flash cards,
study- and practice-mode assessment tests, and review-oriented quick
reference sheets. Together, these elements help you assess your
knowledge of CCDA and CCDP concepts and focus your practice on
those areas where you need the most help. This book was developed in
cooperation with the Cisco Internet Learning Solutions Group. Cisco
Press books are the only self-study books authorized by Cisco Systems
for CCDA and CCDP exam preparation.

Cisco and Cisco Press present this material in a text-based format to
provide another learning vehicle for our customers and the broader user
community, in general. Although a publication does not duplicate the
instructor-led or e-learning environment, we acknowledge that not
everyone responds to the same delivery mechanism in the same way. It is
our intent that presenting this material through a Cisco Press publication
will enhance the transfer of knowledge to a broad audience of
networking professionals.

Cisco Press presents existing and future practice test products through
these Flash Cards and Exam Practice Packs to help achieve the Cisco
Internet Learning Solutions Group principal objectives: to educate the
Cisco community of networking professionals and to enable that
community to build and maintain reliable, scalable networks. The Cisco
Career Certifications and classes that support these certifications are
directed at meeting these objectives through a disciplined approach to
progressive learning. To succeed on the Cisco Career Certifications
exams and in your daily job as a Cisco certified professional, we
recommend a blended learning solution that combines instructor-led, e-
learning, and self-study training with hands-on experience. Cisco Systems
has created an authorized Cisco Learning Partner program to provide you
with the most highly qualified instruction and invaluable hands-on
experience in lab and simulation environments. To learn more about Cisco
Learning Partner programs that are available in your area, please visit
http://www.cisco.com/go/authorized/training.

The books Cisco Press creates, in partnership with Cisco Systems, meet
the same standards for content quality that are demanded of the courses
and certifications. We hope that you will find this and subsequent Cisco
Press certification and training publications valuable as you build your
networking knowledge base.

Thomas M. Kelly
Vice President, Internet Learning Solutions Group
Cisco Systems, Inc.
December 2003

Introduction

Since the Cisco Systems, Inc. career certification programs were announced in 1998, they have been the most sought-after and prestigious certifications in the networking industry. Achieving one's CCDA certification demonstrates a fundamental ability to design networks based on Cisco products and technologies. The CCDP certification signifies advanced competency in network design.

Notorious for being some of the most difficult certifications in the networking industry, Cisco exams can cause the ill-prepared much stress. Unlike other certification exams, the Cisco exams require that students truly understand the material rather than simply memorizing answers. This pack is designed to help you assess whether you are prepared to pass the CCDA (DESGN—Designing for Cisco Internetwork Solutions, exam 640-861) and/or CCDP (ARCH—Designing Cisco Network Architectures, exam 642-871) exams. It contains flash cards that assist in memorization, quick reference sheets that provide condensed exam information, and a powerful exam engine to help you determine whether you are prepared for the actual exam.

The Purpose of Flash Cards

For years, flash cards have been recognized as a quick and effective study aid. They have been used to complement classroom training and significantly boost memory retention.

The flash cards in this pack serve as a final preparation tool for the CCDA and CCDP exams. Note that content for the BSCI and BCMSN exams are also part of the CCDP certification track; material on these exams is presented in the *CCNP Flash Cards and Exam Practice Pack* (ISBN 1-58720-091-0), which is also available from Cisco Press. Therefore, this publication does not repeat BSCI and BCMSN content.

These flash cards work best when used in conjunction with official study aids for the CCDA DESGN and CCDP ARCH exams. Table I-1 presents the required exams and recommended study for CCDA and CCDP certification. Note that these cards and quick reference sheets can be used in conjunction with any other CCDA and CCDP exam preparation book or course of study. They might also be useful to you as a quick desk or field reference guide. A composite exam, 642-891, which covers BSCI and BCMSN, can also be taken in place of the individual BSCI and BCMSN exams.

Table I-1   *Exams and Courses Required to Achieve CCDA/CCDP Certifications*

Certification	Exam Number	Name	Course Most Closely Matching Exam Requirements
CCDA	#640-861	CCDA Exam	Designing for Cisco Internetwork Solutions (DESGN)
CCDP*	#642-801	BSCI Exam	Building Scalable Cisco Internetworks (BSCI)
	#642-811	BCMSN Exam	Building Cisco Multilayer Switched Networks (BCMSN)
	#642-871	ARCH Exam	Designing Cisco Network Service Architectures (ARCH)

*Note that a valid CCDA certification is required to obtain CCDP certification.

Whom These Flash Cards Are Intended For

These flash cards are designed for network administrators, network designers, and any professional or student looking to advance his career by achieving Cisco CCDA and/or CCDP certifications.

How to Use These Flash Cards

Review one section at a time, reading each flash card until you can answer it correctly on your own. When you can correctly answer every card in a given section, move on to the next section.

These flash cards are a condensed form of study and review. Do not rush through each section. The amount of time you spend reviewing the cards directly affects how long you will be able to retain the information needed to pass the test. Review each section as a final refresher a couple of days before your exam.

Although these flash cards are designed as a final-stage study aid (30 days before the exam), they can also be used in the following situations:

- **Pre-study evaluation**—Before charting out your course of study, read one or two questions at the beginning and end of each section to gauge your competence in the specific areas.

- **Reinforcement of key topics**—After you complete your study of each area, read through the answer cards (on the left side of the pages) to identify key topics and reinforce concepts.

- **Identifying areas for last-minute review**—In the days before an exam, review the study cards and carefully note your areas of weakness. Concentrate your remaining study time on these areas.

- **Post-study quiz**—By flipping through this book at random and viewing the questions on the right side of the pages, you can randomize your self-quiz to ensure that you are prepared in all areas.

- **Desk reference or field guide to core concepts (quick reference sheets section only)**—Networking professionals, sales representatives, and help-desk technicians alike can benefit from a handy, simple-to-navigate book that outlines the major topics aligned with networking principles and CCDA and CCDP certifications.

Quick Reference Sheets

At the conclusion of each part of this book, you can find more than 55 total pages of quick reference sheets. These sheets serve as both a study guide for the CCDA and CCDP exams, and as a companion reference to the text. For readers who seek CCDA and/or CCDP certifications, these quick reference sheets are well suited to reinforce the concepts learned in the text, rather than as a sole source of information. For readers who have either already obtained CCDA and/or CCDP certification or simply need a basic overview, these sheets can serve as a standalone reference. A complete set of these sheets can also be printed from the enclosed CD-ROM.

What the CD-ROM Includes

The CD-ROM includes copies of the 350+ flash cards and quick reference sheets presented in the physical book. It also includes an electronic version of the flash cards that runs on most Windows and Palm platforms. The CD-ROM allows you to randomize your study by shuffling the flash cards. It also includes a powerful 550-question practice test engine that simulates each of the CCDA and CCDP exams. The practice test engine familiarizes you with the format of the exams and reinforces the knowledge you need to pass them.

Special Features

You might notice that some flash cards on the CD-ROM provide pointers to the quick reference sheets included on PDF to provide you with an additional mode of reviewing. Additional CD-ROM features include the following:

- Palm OS format, which enables you to study for the CCDA and CCDP exams on your Palm.

- The ability to shuffle the flash cards and the option to review custom sets that focus your study on difficult terms, basic concepts, or a "final exam."

Exam Registration

The CCDA DESGN and CCDP ARCH exams are computer-based exams, with multiple-choice, fill-in-the-blank, and list-in-order questions. You can take the exam at any Pearson VUE (http://www.pearsonvue.com) or Prometric (http://www.2test.com) testing center. Your testing center can tell you the exact length of the exam. Be aware that when you register for the exam, you might be told to allow a certain amount of time to take the exam that is longer than the testing time indicated by the testing software when you begin. This is because VUE and Prometric want you to allow for some time to get settled and take the tutorial about the testing engine.

Part I

CCDA-DESGN

Section 1
Network Design Methodologies

Section 2
Evaluating Organizational Policies and Procedures

Section 3
Examining Customer Requirements

Section 4
Characterizing the Existing Network

Section 5
Implementing the Design Methodology

Section 6
Network Hierarchies

Section 7
Modular Network Designs

Section 8
Switching Design Considerations

Section 9
Campus Design Details

Section 10
Enterprise WAN Solutions

Section 11
IP Addressing

Section 12
Routing Protocols

Section 13
Security

Section 14
Voice

Section 15
Network Management

CCDA-DESGN Quick Reference Sheets

Section 1

Network Design Methodologies

As the importance of networks has increased, so has their complexity and the demands placed on network professionals. Network designers are certainly no exception.

When approaching a new design engagement, designers today must have solid and well-designed network design methodologies from which to choose. These methodologies not only simplify the task of designing complex networks, but they can also improve the overall end design and ensure that the design meets the client organization's business and organizational needs.

This section's flash cards ensure that you are familiar with the planning, design, implementation, operation, and optimization methodology that you can use to derive a design methodology. They also expose you to decision tables and review the value of these tools when designing networks.

Question 1

What does the *P* stand for in the PDIOO life cycle?

Question 2

Cisco recommends that a particular design methodology be used. This methodology follows and is derived from PDIOO. What is the first of the design methodology's eight steps?

Question 1 Answer

In the PDIOO life cycle, *P* stands for planning. *D* is design; *I* is implementation; *O* is operation; and *O* is optimization.

Question 2 Answer

The first step in the design methodology is to identify the customer requirements.

Question 3

Cisco recommends that you follow a specific design methodology when designing a network. This methodology consists of eight steps. What is the last step in this recommended design methodology?

Network Design Methodologies

Question 4

What is an advantage to the use of the top-down design approach?

Network Design Methodologies

Question 3 Answer

The last step in the design methodology is to monitor and potentially redesign portions of the network.

Question 4 Answer

The top-down approach to designing the network features several potential advantages, including the following:

- Centers around meeting customer requirements
- Provides for an easy-to-comprehend "picture" of the network to clients
- Typically meets the client's current and future requirements by incorporating scalability

Question 5

What is the purpose of a decision table?

Question 6

Give a specific example of when a decision table might prove useful in a design engagement.

Question 5 Answer

A decision table allows you to make a systematic decision when multiple potential solutions exist for a given problem.

Question 6 Answer

You might use a decision table when deciding on the following:

- Routing protocol
- Type of security
- Physical topology
- WAN technology
- Switching technology
- Redundancy methods

Section 2

Evaluating Organizational Policies and Procedures

Many network designers forget to analyze the organizational policies and procedures that help define a business. These factors can often be as critical as purely technical factors. This section reviews the key aspects a network designer should be familiar with, including organizational models, policies, and procedures.

Question 1

Why is a network organizational model based on vertical integration often less beneficial than a horizontal integration model?

Question 2

Name at least two of the network organizational architecture components.

Question 1 Answer

In an organizational model that is based on vertical integration, almost all of the production comes from within the organization. Based upon the horizontal integration model, modern internetworking leverages partnerships with entities outside the organization. These partnerships can dramatically increase competitive advantage.

Question 2 Answer

The network organizational architectures components include

- Applications
- Enabling network solutions
- Prerequisite systems
- Network infrastructure including intelligent network services (content networking, storage networking, Voice over IP)

Question 3

Name an organizationally specific policy that could dramatically impact network design decisions.

Evaluating Organizational Policies

Question 4

The network that a designer recommends should help the organization achieve its business goals. This is accomplished by adhering to the network's guidelines, such as scalability, manageability, and efficiency. Name at least two additional guidelines.

Evaluating Organizational Policies

Question 3 Answer

Examples of organizationally specific policies that could impact network design decisions include vendor preferences, technology preferences, and employment policies.

Question 4 Answer

The network should contribute to all of the organizational goals by adhering to the following:

- Functionality
- Scalability
- Availability
- Performance
- Manageability
- Efficiency

Section 3

Examining Customer Requirements

Carefully extracting the customer requirements before engaging in a network design is critical for a customer. It is important to examine the project's scope. Is it going to be an entirely new network? Is the design engagement to simply replace one small portion of the network? Is the goal to add new functionality to the network? For example, perhaps Voice over IP functionality is required.

Examination of the organizational goals and the network design goals is also critical. It is important to ensure that the design helps the organization meet these goals. You should not recommend technologies simply for the sake of recommending new technologies.

You should also examine organizational constraints, including such factors as the budget, personnel, and scheduling issues.

Finally, you must carefully examine the organization's technical requirements and constraints. Technical constraints might include bandwidth availability and application compatibility.

Question 1

What is an example of a question that should be asked regarding the scope of a network design?

Question 2

Which of the OSI model layers deals with the design of routing and addressing issues?

Question 1 Answer

Following are possible questions that should be asked during a scope analysis:

- Is the design for a single network segment?
- Is the design for a single network module?
- Is the design for a subset of the overall network?
- Is the design for the entire network?
- Is the design's purpose to add a single network function?
- Is the design's purpose to add entire network functionality?

Question 2 Answer

The Open System Interconnection (OSI) model's network layer designs routing and addressing issues. The OSI model's application layer includes the design of voice over IP, for example. Physical and data link layer design decisions include fiber versus copper and ATM versus Frame Relay, for example.

Question 3

After you determine the organizational goals during the design engagement, what should you do next?

Question 4

After you determine the technical goals during the design engagement, what should you do next?

Question 3 Answer

After determining the organizational goals, you should determine the organizational constraints.

Question 4 Answer

After determining the technical goals, you should determine the technical constraints.

Question 5

Provide an example of an organizational goal that might be discovered during the design engagement.

Examining Customer Requirements

Question 6

Provide an example of an organizational constraint.

Examining Customer Requirements

Question 5 Answer

The following are examples of organizational goals:

- Increase revenue
- Increase profits
- Shorten development cycles
- Increase competitiveness
- Add new customers
- Enhance productivity
- Improve customer service
- Improve customer satisfaction
- Improve the sharing of data inside and outside of the organization

Question 6 Answer

The following are examples of organizational constraints:

- Budget
- Personnel
- Policies
- Scheduling

Question 7

Provide an example of a planned application in a design engagement.

Question 8

Provide an example of a planned network service in a design engagement.

Question 7 Answer

Planned applications for an organization might include the following:

- E-mail
- Groupware
- Voice networking
- WWW
- Video on Demand
- Database

Question 8 Answer

Planned network services might include

- Security
- Quality of service (QoS)
- Network Management
- High Availability (Service Level Offerings)
- IP Multicast

Question 9

Provide several examples of technical goals that an organization might possess.

Examining
Customer
Requirements

Question 10

Provide an example of a technical constraint that might be discovered during a design engagement.

Examining
Customer
Requirements

Question 9 Answer

Following are examples of technical goals that an organization might possess:

- Simplify network management
- Improve scalability
- Replace legacy equipment
- Improve availability
- Increase security
- Improve performance
- Improve reliability

Question 10 Answer

The following are examples of technical constraints that might be discovered:

- Legacy equipment
- Bandwidth availability
- Application compatibility
- Personnel qualifications

Section 4

Characterizing the Existing Network

Yet another critical task early in the design engagement is for the network designer to carefully analyze and characterize the existing network. This is, of course, provided that there is an existing network!

Careful analysis of the existing network culminates in the creation of a summary report, which includes information about the current health of the network and recommendations for new equipment and technologies to meet the organization's business and technical goals.

Question 1

Name at least one step in which a designer should engage when characterizing the existing customer network.

Question 2

List four components a network designer should collect during the network audit of an existing network.

Question 1 Answer

The following are the three general steps a designer should engage in when characterizing the existing network:

- Collect customer input
- Perform a network audit
- Perform traffic analysis

Question 2 Answer

The network audit of the existing network might include the following components:

- Detailed list of devices in the network
- Hardware specifications of devices in the network
- Software specifications of devices in the network
- Device configurations
- Output from various auditing tools
- Expandability information for devices
- Utilization statistics for devices

Question 3

Name at least one network auditing recommendation.

Question 4

You are interested in using a Cisco network-auditing tool that can provide topology information and details about hardware and software configurations in an automated fashion. What tool should you use?

Question 3 Answer

Network auditing recommendations include

- Leverage existing auditing tools, if such tools exist.
- Introduce additional tools as needed.
- Minor changes to the network might be necessary for collecting the required data; when complete, log these changes and reverse.
- Automated auditing approaches should be employed in large networks.
- Create summary reports based on detailed information.

Question 4 Answer

CiscoWorks provides dynamic topology information for Cisco devices through use of the Campus Manager application. Campus Manager can work in conjunction with Resource Manager Essentials, which provides details about hardware and software configurations.

Question 5

You are performing a manual network audit of an existing customer network. What command should you use on a Cisco router to determine the exact version of IOS that is in place and the hardware modules that are installed?

Question 6

You are performing a manual network audit of an existing customer network. What command should you use on a Cisco router to determine the extent of CPU utilization?

Question 5 Answer

You should use the *show version* command to determine the exact version of software and the network modules in use. The *show version* command also provides the amount of uptime for the device.

Question 6 Answer

You should use the *show processes cpu* command to gain valuable information about device CPU utilization. To increase the effectiveness of this command, consider examining the output over a period of samples. Also, to view non-zero processes, use *show processes cpu | exclude 0.0*.

Question 7

You are engaged in a manual analysis of network traffic in an existing customer network. You would like to rely on IOS-based tools and, specifically, you would like to display statistics for all interfaces that are broken down by protocol and an average 30-second bit rate. What tool should you use?

Question 8

Based on a characterization of the existing customer network, name at least two components that should be included in the summary report.

Question 7 Answer

Thanks to the NBAR Protocol Discovery feature, the Cisco IOS NBAR tool provides such statistics.

Question 8 Answer

The summary report document should summarize the results of characterizing the existing network. It should do the following:

- Describe the required software features
- Describe possible problems
- Identify actions needed to modify the network
- Influence the customer in terms of requirements and changes

Section 5

Implementing the Design Methodology

It is important to follow a structured approach when you are ready to implement the design you have worked so hard on. If the design is very complex, consisting of many steps, you should implement the steps separately and carefully. There should also be detailed implementation documentation.

You should consider a pilot or prototype to prove that your design works. You should also possess a detailed design document.

Question 1

Why is it beneficial to implement each step of the design separately if the steps are complex?

Implementing the Design Methodology

Question 2

A network design implementation should consist of several phases, each of which should consist of separate steps. Name at least two components that each step should contain.

Implementing the Design Methodology

Question 1 Answer

It is beneficial to implement each complex step of the design separately for two main reasons:

- To reduce troubleshooting in the event of failures
- To reduce the time to roll-back in the result of failure

Question 2 Answer

Each step should contain the following elements:

- Description
- Reference to appropriate design documents
- Detailed implementation guidelines
- Detailed roll-back guidelines
- Estimated time required for implementation

Question 3

You are interested in proving your design concept to the customer of your design engagement. You plan on testing and verifying the redesign in an isolated network at your facility. What is this type of proof of concept called?

Question 4

Name at least four components you should include in the final design document.

Question 3 Answer

When you test and verify a redesign in an isolated network, you are engaging in what is called a prototype network.

A pilot network tests and verifies the design before it is launched.

Question 4 Answer

The final design document should include the following components:

- Description
- Reference to appropriate design documents
- Detailed implementation guidelines
- Detailed roll-back guidelines
- Estimated time required for implementation

Section 6

Network Hierarchies

Today's networks are complex and sophisticated. To properly design modern networks, designers can simplify the process by using network models. Cisco proposed an early model—the network hierarchical model—that is still used today. This model allows for a simplification of complex networks and more efficient design engagements.

Question 1

What are the three layers of the Cisco hierarchical network model?

Question 2

Which layer of the Cisco hierarchical network model features speed as its biggest focus?

Question 1 Answer

This Cisco hierarchical network model consists of three layers, which include the following:

- Access layer
- Distribution layer
- Core layer

Question 2 Answer

The core layer is most concerned with speed. In fact, security and other such measures are typically not employed in this layer to ensure that packets move as quickly as possible.

Question 3

Which layer of the Cisco hierarchical network model is most likely to feature QoS controls?

Question 4

Redundancy is most important at which layer of the Cisco hierarchical network model?

Question 3 Answer

The distribution layer most often features QoS measures. This ensures that certain types of traffic take precedence over other types of traffic.

Question 4 Answer

Redundancy is critical at the core layer of the Cisco hierarchical network model. This ensures that failures do not have a major impact on network connectivity. While this is the correct certification response, remember that redundancy can be critical at all layers of the model—especially the distribution layer.

Question 5

At which layer of the Cisco hierarchical network model are you most likely to find authentication to take place?

Question 6

Which layer of the Cisco hierarchical network model is most likely to feature Layer 2 switching?

Question 5 Answer

The access layer frequently features authentication to ensure that network users are actually permitted to use the network. While this is the optimal certification response, understand that authentication also takes place in the distribution layer, especially in the case of VPNs.

Question 6 Answer

The access layer of the Cisco network hierarchical model most often features Layer 2 switching. These low-cost switches provide full duplex network access to clients.

Question 7

Which layer of the Cisco hierarchical network model is most likely to feature Layer 3 switching?

Question 7 Answer

The distribution layer of the Cisco hierarchical network model often features Layer 3 switching. This permits packets to be routed to other areas of the network or beyond.

Section 7
Modular Network Designs

The Cisco hierarchical network model is a powerful tool for network designers. However, as networks have grown more complex and sophisticated, the model has had its problems. Specifically, network designers who rely solely on this model find it too difficult to scale networks based on the simple blueprint of access, distribution, and core.

Cisco has created a much more elaborate and modular network design model to assist the modern Cisco network designer. It is called the Enterprise Composite Network Model and it does not abandon the earlier hierarchical network model. The earlier hierarchical network model integrates nicely into the new model's network, as needed.

Question 1

What are the Enterprise Composite Network Model's three main functional areas?

Question 2

What are the four major modules that make up the Enterprise Campus major functional area of the Enterprise Composite Network Model?

Question 1 Answer

The three main functional areas of the Enterprise Composite Network Model are

- Enterprise Campus
- Enterprise Edge
- Service Provider Edge

Question 2 Answer

The Enterprise Campus major functional area consists of the following modules:

- Campus infrastructure
- Network management
- Server farm
- Edge distribution

Question 3

What are the three submodules of the Campus Infrastructure module of the Enterprise Composite Network Model?

Question 4

The Network Management module is a module of the Enterprise Campus major functional area. Name at least three functions that this module performs.

Question 3 Answer

The Enterprise Composite Network Model's Campus Infrastructure module consists of the following three submodules:

- Building access
- Building distribution
- Campus backbone

Question 4 Answer

The Network Management module can perform the following functions for an organization:

- Intrusion detection
- System logging
- Authentication
- Network monitoring
- Configuration management
- Terminal services (remote control)

Question 5

Name at least three examples of servers that might be found in the Enterprise Campus major functional area's server farm module.

Question 6

What is the purpose of the Enterprise Campus major functional area's Edge Distribution module?

Question 5 Answer

Many types of servers can exist in the Server Farm module of the Enterprise Campus major functional area. Some of these servers include the following:

- E-mail
- Application
- File and Print
- DNS
- Database
- IP telephony

Question 6 Answer

The Edge Distribution module of the Enterprise Campus major functional area aggregates the connectivity from the Enterprise Edge and routes the traffic into the campus backbone submodule.

Question 7

What are the four modules that comprise the Enterprise Edge functional area of the Enterprise Composite Network module?

Modular Network Designs

Question 8

What three modules are commonly found in the Service Provider Edge functional area?

Modular Network Designs

Question 7 Answer

The four modules that comprise the Enterprise Edge functional area of the Enterprise Composite Network module are

- E-commerce
- Internet connectivity
- Remote access and VPN
- WAN

Question 8 Answer

Three modules that are commonly found in the Service Provider Edge functional area are

- Internet service provider
- PSTN (Public Switched Telephone Network)
- Frame Relay/Asynchronous Transfer Mode (ATM)

Section 8

Switching Design Considerations

After you design the perfect modular network, you are not finished making important decisions—and these decisions are in the campus module alone. You must decide on the appropriate physical layer implementation and other such considerations.

This section reminds you of key factors you should consider when designing the campus module.

Question 1

Name at least three major campus design decisions that are typical for a design engagement.

Question 2

Which is more expensive to install and implement as a physical layer transmission medium: copper or fiber?

Question 1 Answer

You must meet several major decision areas when designing scalable and efficient campus networks. These design considerations might include the following:

- Geography
- Applications
- Transmission media
- Switched or shared
- L2 or L3 switching

Question 2 Answer

Fiber is more expensive to implement than copper. This is primarily because strict optical cable coupling requirements must be met.

Question 3

What is long reach Ethernet, and upon what physical medium does it rely?

Question 4

If you should opt for a switched design (as opposed to a shared design) in your campus network, you achieve the benefit of larger network diameters. Why?

Question 3 Answer

Long Reach Ethernet (LRE) relies upon copper media. As its name implies, it permits longer distances than traditional Ethernet. Specifically, it permits runs of up to 1.5 km. It is typically used as a distribution technology for broadband building access.

Question 4 Answer

Larger network diameters are possible with switched designs because no collision detection algorithm is necessary.

Question 5

You are interested in performing load sharing in your campus network design. You are specifically interested in engaging in IP load sharing between specific ports based on IP addresses. Should you engage in Layer 2 or Layer 3 switching?

Question 6

You are considering recommending the use of PortFast in a campus network design. Where is this Spanning Tree protocol enhancement typically implemented? Why?

Question 5 Answer

L3 switching permits load sharing based on IP addresses. Any ports can be used to implement this sharing behavior. L2 switching permits limited load sharing based on VLANs across uplink ports only.

Question 6 Answer

PortFast allows for a much faster transition from the blocking state to the forwarding state for a switch port. Because PortFast should be used to connect end systems to the network, it is typically implemented in the campus network's wiring closet (the access layer).

Question 7

You are recommending the use of UplinkFast in a campus network design. Where is this Spanning Tree protocol enhancement typically implemented?

Question 8

Where would you implement BackboneFast in a campus design?

Question 7 Answer

UplinkFast is a wiring closet switch (access layer) technology that permits the quick failover to an alternate uplink when a direct link failure is detected.

Question 8 Answer

BackboneFast allows for a faster convergence following the failure of a remote link in the topology. BackboneFast must be implemented on all switches in the campus.

Section 9

Campus Design Details

What specific considerations must you manage as campus network designer? This section ensures that you know these and tests your knowledge of campus module by campus module, from the access layer to the server farm.

Question 1

You are going to engage in a detailed design of the campus network for a business client. In which campus modules would performance be the biggest concern?

Question 2

You are going to engage in a detailed design of the campus network for a business client. In which module of the campus would scalability be the biggest concern?

Question 1 Answer

Performance is the greatest concern in the server farm module or the backbone (core) module.

Question 2 Answer

Scalability is a large concern for the access module of the campus network. This module must be able to easily grow to support additional users who might require network connectivity.

Question 3

What is the 80/20 rule of network traffic patterns?

Question 4

What is the technology described by the following statement:

This is a Cisco proprietary solution implemented in some Cisco switches that permits the switch to learn multicast receiver registration information from Cisco routers.

Question 3 Answer

The 80/20 rule of network traffic flows states that 80 percent of the traffic remains within the local workgroup. Only 20 percent is destined for remote systems. This is now considered a legacy design because modern networks feature much more remote resources. The modern traffic pattern follows a 20/80 rule.

Question 4 Answer

This is a description of the Cisco Group Management Protocol (CGMP).

Question 5

You are interested in controlling traffic flows in your Enterprise WAN, which consists of Frame Relay connections between several campus segments. You want to drop or lower the priority of a frame that resides outside of a traffic profile that you define. Is this a description of traffic shaping or traffic policing?

Campus Design Details

Question 6

Name at least two major considerations a network designer should have when designing the access layer of a campus network.

Campus Design Details

Question 5 Answer

Traffic policing drops or lowers the priority of frames that fall outside the policy that you define. You should contrast this with traffic shaping that controls transmission rates through the buffering of traffic.

Question 6 Answer

The designer should have the following considerations:

- Number of ports required
- Physical layer cabling
- Performance required
- Redundancy required
- Speeds required
- VLANs and STP configuration
- Additional features (QoS, multicast, etc.)

Question 7

Name at least two major considerations a network designer should have when designing a campus network's distribution layer.

Question 8

Name at least two major considerations a network designer should have when designing a campus network's core layer.

Question 7 Answer

The following considerations should be the focus of the distribution layer module:

- L2 or L3 switching
- Performance required
- Number of ports required
- Redundancy required
- Additional features
- Manageability required

Question 8 Answer

The following considerations should be the focus of the core layer module:

- L2 or L3 switching
- Performance required
- Number of ports required
- Redundancy required

Question 9

Name at least two options for connecting servers to the network in a server farm campus module design.

Question 10

Name at least two types of attacks a designer should consider when designing the Edge Distribution module.

Question 9 Answer

Servers can connect to the network in several ways, including the following:

- Single NIC
- Dual NIC
- Server load-balancing switch

Question 10 Answer

Designers must be aware of the following types of attacks:

- Unauthorized access
- IP spoofing
- Network reconnaissance
- Packet sniffers

Question 11

Name a disadvantage found with the single L2 VLAN core design.

Question 12

Name at least one advantage of the dual-path L3 core design.

Question 11 Answer

Disadvantages to the single L2 VLAN core design include the following:

- No broadcast/multicast controls
- L3 peering issues in the distribution layer

Question 12 Answer

Advantages to this design model include the following:

- Two equal-cost paths to every network destination
- Quick recovery from link failures
- Double link capacity

Section 10

Enterprise WAN Solutions

Today, organizations can implement a variety of WAN solutions. WAN components are a key part of the design because they represent a huge portion of the expense of designing and continuously running a network.

This section ensures that you are knowledgeable about traditional WAN design options and new and emerging technologies.

Question 1

ISDN falls into which category of traditional WAN technologies?

Question 2

Which emerging WAN technology offers high-speed data transfers for the SOHO WAN site using traditional telephone copper lines?

Question 1 Answer

ISDN and asynchronous serial dialup connections are perfect examples of circuit-switched traditional WAN technologies.

Question 2 Answer

Digital subscriber line (DSL) permits high-speed transfers for SOHO WAN sites. Typically, upload speeds do not equal download speeds, however. This is true for the most common form of small business, residential installations of a technology called Asynchronous DSL (ADSL).

Question 3

Describe the concept known as jitter.

Question 4

**Which WAN technology is noted for trans-
mission speeds of 15 Mbps?**

Question 3 Answer

Jitter is variable delay that the network experiences. This can be damaging for clear voice transmissions. Voice calls are intolerant of variations in the delay within the network.

Question 4 Answer

Long Reach Ethernet dramatically expands the maximum cable runs that can be used for transmissions and features a transmission speed of 15 Mbps.

Question 5

Which queuing mechanism supported on Cisco routers features 16 interface output queues and guarantees some level of service to all traffic?

Question 6

Name at least two issues that occur when a full mesh Frame Relay topology is chosen.

Question 5 Answer

Custom queuing uses 16 interface output queues. This method of software queuing provides some level of service to all traffic and is therefore often considered better than priority queuing, which can starve some types of traffic.

Question 6 Answer

Full mesh Frame Relay topologies do have advantages, but they also have disadvantages, including the following:

- The large number of virtual circuits can be quite expensive.
- Several packets might have to be replicated in the topology.
- Configurations can be quite complex.

Question 7

Describe a shadow PVC as it is used for WAN backup.

Question 8

What is the main difference between ADSL and SDSL?

Question 7 Answer

A shadow PVC is a secondary permanent virtual circuit that is implemented from the provider to backup a primary WAN connection. Typically, there is no charge for this second PVC. Often, a charge for the second link is levied should usage exceed a certain threshold.

Question 8 Answer

ADSL often features dramatic differences in transmission speeds upstream and downstream. SDSL features identical speeds upstream and downstream.

Question 9

Name two of the three different typical wireless implementations.

Question 10

What are the two main methods of tunneling private networks over the public Internet.

Question 9 Answer

Typical implementations of wireless technologies include the following:

- Broadband fixed wireless
- Mobile wireless
- Wireless LAN

Question 10 Answer

The two main methods are

- IPSec
- GRE

Question 11

Describe MPLS.

Question 11 Answer

With MPLS, packets are labeled for quick and efficient forwarding through an MPLS network.

Section 11

IP Addressing

CCDA-DESGN

A large part of designing a TCP/IP based network properly involves ensuring that TCP/IP addressing is done correctly. This not only includes planning the IP addresses carefully, but also deciding how the addresses are to actually be implemented on the equipment.

The CCDA candidate must also have a firm grasp of IPv6, since more and more networks are supporting this next generation IP addressing technology. This section reviews these issues—including key points regarding IPv6.

Question 1

Provide an example of a flat address that is used in modern computer networking.

Question 2

What is the meaning of the following statement:

IP addresses are hierarchical.

Question 1 Answer

A Media Access Control (MAC) address is an example of a flat address that is used in modern computer networks. MAC addresses are used for Layer 2 addressing in Ethernet networks. These address uniquely identify a system on the network.

Question 2 Answer

This means that IP addresses are composed of multiple parts, each having a specific meaning. IP addresses are composed of a network portion and a host portion.

Question 3

How many bits does an IP address contain, and how is it typically presented?

Question 4

The following IP address and subnet mask are used on a workstation in a subnet of the network.

IP Address: 172.16.2.100

Subnet Mast: 255.255.255.240

How many total host addresses are available in the subnet?

Question 3 Answer

An IP address consists of 32 bits. It is typically presented in dotted decimal form. For example: 10.24.65.128.

Question 4 Answer

Given the subnet mask of 255.255.255.240, 28 bits are used for the network identification. This leaves four bits for host addressing. 2 raised to the 4th power is 16, minus 2 equals 14. Therefore, there are 14 total available host addresses in the subnet.

Question 5

What is the range of possible values in the first octet for a Class B IP address?

Question 6

List at least two questions that should be asked before designing a network's IP addressing.

Question 5 Answer

128–191

Class A—first octet starts with 0; 0 to 127

Class B—first octet starts with 10; 128–191

Class C—first octet starts with 110; 192–233

Class D—first octet starts with 1110; 224–239

Class E—first octet starts with 1111; 240–255

Question 6 Answer

It is important to ask all the following questions:

- How large is the network?
- How many locations exist?
- What are the IP addressing requirements for locations?
- What class and how many networks can be obtained from the public number authority?

Question 7

Name at least two private address ranges.

Question 8

What technology allows multiple internal addresses to be converted at a router into addresses that are usable on the public Internet?

Question 7 Answer

The private IP address ranges are

- 10.0.0.0/8
- 172.16.0.0/12
- 192.168.0.0/16

Question 8 Answer

Network Address Translation allows internal network addresses to be translated into global Internet addresses. Port address translation allows multiple internal addresses to be mapped to a single external address.

Question 9

A popular characterization of dynamic routing protocols examines whether a routing update contains subnet mask information. What is this characterization called, and which type of routing includes the subnet mask information?

IP Addressing

Question 10

How many bits does an IPv6 address contain, and how is it typically presented?

IP Addressing

Question 9 Answer

The characterization is classless versus classful. Classless routing protocols include the subnet mask information in routing updates. These protocols are considered second generation and can use VLSM.

Question 10 Answer

An IPv6 IP address contains 128 bits. They are typically presented as hexadecimal numbers separated by colons.

Question 11

What is the meaning of two colons (::) in an IPv6 address?

Question 12

What field is used in an IPv6 header to facilitate special handling, such as QoS?

Question 11 Answer

Two colons can be used to represent successive hexadecimal fields of zeros. This can be done once within an IP address.

Question 12 Answer

The Flow Label field is used to label packets for special handling.

Question 13

What IPv6 address scope type allows for a station to send data to the nearest interface with the configured address type?

Question 14

Name at least two transition strategies for IPv6.

Question 13 Answer

The new anycast address scope permits this behavior. It can be considered one to nearest behavior.

Question 14 Answer

Following are the three major mechanisms that should assist with the deployment and transition to IPv6:

- **Dual Stack**—System runs both IPv4 and IPv6.
- **Tunneling**—Encapsulates IPv6 packets into IPv4 packets, and vice versa.
- **Translation**—One protocol is translated into another to facilitate communications.

Section 12

Routing Protocols

A variety of routing solutions can be implemented in Cisco equipment. Routing protocols can be categorized by the following solutions, to name a few:

- Static versus dynamic
- Flat versus hierarchical
- Distance vector versus link state
- Classful versus classless

This variety in the world of routing protocols ensures that network designers must face tough decisions when planning for the deployment of a particular routing protocol for a particular network. This section recalls these issues and ensures that you understand the fundamental differences in routing protocols so you can make these key decisions effectively.

Question 1

Name at least two cases where static routing is appropriate within a network design.

Question 2

You are considering using static routes in a stub area configuration with a network. What are two advantages that exist through the use of a static route in this design?

Question 1 Answer

Static routing is appropriate in the following cases:

- The network is small and not complex; the network also has a very slow rate of expansion or change.

- The network consists of a main larger network with one or more stub networks.

- The network should include special features, such as dial-on-demand routing.

Question 2 Answer

By using a static route with a stub network, the following advantages exist:

- Dynamic routing protocol control information is not used on the link to the stub, or in the stub network; this reduces the amount of routing protocol traffic the network must carry.

- Smaller routing tables are present in routers with the stub and central networks.

- Low end routers can be used in the stub network.

- Processor requirements for routers are lower.

Question 3

Which of the following routing protocols are considered distance vector?

- **EIGRP**
- **OSPF**
- **IS-IS**
- **BGP**
- **RIP v1**
- **IGRP**
- **RIP v2**

Routing
Protocols

Question 4

Because it is a routing protocol that features the best of distance vector mechanisms and the best of link state mechanisms, it is often considered a hybrid routing protocol. Which is it?

Routing
Protocols

Question 3 Answer

BGP, RIP v1 and v2, and IGRP are all considered distance vector routing protocols. EIGRP is considered a hybrid routing protocol.

Question 4 Answer

EIGRP offers the best features of both types of protocols and, as a result, is often considered a hybrid routing protocol.

Question 5

What algorithm does link state routing protocols use to select the best path to a destination?

Routing
Protocols

Question 6

What is the most common Exterior Gateway Protocol in use today, and what is its function?

Routing
Protocols

Question 5 Answer

The common shortest path first, or Dijkstra's algorithm, is used.

Question 6 Answer

BGP Version 4 powers the routing functions of the Internet as we know it today. BGP+ takes over once IPv6 is fully deployed. BGP is responsible for routing between separate autonomous systems.

Question 7

What default metrics does EIGRP use?

Question 8

What is the default metric used by OSPF? From what is this value derived, by default?

Question 7 Answer

The default metrics used by EIGRP are bandwidth and delay.

Question 8 Answer

The default metric used by OSPF is cost. By default, this metric is derived from bandwidth.

Question 9

What default metric does RIP use?

Routing
Protocols

Question 10

Which type of routing protocol converges faster: distance vector or link state? Why?

Routing
Protocols

Question 9 Answer

The default metric used by RIP is hop count.

Question 10 Answer

Link state routing protocols converge faster than distance vector protocols because they instantly propagate route updates, while distance vector technologies rely on a periodic update. This statement remains true when the distance vector routing protocols use their default timers, of course.

Question 11

What is the main difference between a classful routing protocol and a classless routing protocol?

Question 12

Describe variable length subnet masking.

Question 11 Answer

A classful routing protocol does not send the subnet mask information with routing updates. A classless routing protocol includes this information.

Question 12 Answer

Variable length subnet masking allows the administrator to assign different subnet masks to different parts of the network. This allows for more efficient use of available IP address space, and for more hierarchical-based network designs. As a result, summarization can be performed, and more efficient dynamic routing is achieved.

Question 13

Which type of routing supports VSLM: classful or classless?

Question 14

Which of the following routing protocols are classless routing protocols?

- IGRP
- EIGRP
- RIP v1
- RIP v2
- OSPF
- BGP
- IS-IS

Question 13 Answer

Classless routing protocols support VLSM.

Question 14 Answer

EIGRP, RIP v2, OSPF, BGP, and IS-IS are all classless routing protocols.

Question 15

Name at least two aspects/advantages of on-demand routing.

Question 16

What is the metric, and what is the metric limit with RIP v2?

Question 15 Answer

On-demand routing (ODR) has the following characteristics/
advantages:

- Reduces dynamic routing traffic overhead
- Ideal for hub and spoke topologies
- No IP routing protocol on the stub networks is required
- ODR relies upon CDP

Question 16 Answer

RIP v2 uses hop count as a metric. The hop count limit is 15.

Question 17

Name at least two advantages that RIP v2 has over its RIP v1 counterpart.

Routing
Protocols

Question 18

Which dynamic routing protocol offers built-in support for routing IP and OSI protocols?

Routing
Protocols

Question 17 Answer

The following advantages exist:

- VLSM support
- Multicast, instead of broadcast
- Faster convergence
- Manual route summarization
- Authentication

Question 18 Answer

The IS-IS protocol can do both. It is called Integrated IS-IS when it is used for routing TCP/IP traffic.

Question 19

When BGP is running between routers in a single autonomous system, what is it called?

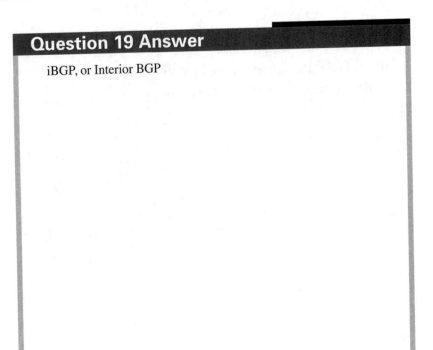

Question 19 Answer

iBGP, or Interior BGP

Section 13

Security

More and more attacks against networks arise every year. Many of these attacks receive major publicity because they cause billions of dollars in damages to corporations and even small businesses. As the leader in networking equipment, Cisco Systems has responded with a powerful SAFE blueprint for securing corporate networks. This section ensures that you are familiar with this blueprint and that you have minimal difficulty answering questions about security in the exam environment.

Question 1

Network security aims to provide data integrity, data confidentiality, and system availability. What is the meaning of data integrity?

Question 2

Many types of attacks involve sending a host a malformed message that is known to cause an error, or overwhelming the host with massive amounts of data. What are these types of attacks typically called?

Question 1 Answer

Data integrity means that the network data is valid and has not been changed or tampered with in any way.

Question 2 Answer

These types of attacks are typically called denial of service attacks.

Question 3

Many attacks involve searching the network for addresses, possible targets, and security gaps. What are these types of attacks typically called?

Question 4

Provide at least two reasons why it so important to physically secure a router or switch.

Question 3 Answer

These attacks are typically called reconnaissance attacks.

Question 4 Answer

It is important to physically secure these devices for the following reasons:

- Console access allows an administrator to override any security that is placed on the device.
- Theft.
- Installation of software directly.
- Installation of new hardware directly.

Question 5

Provide at least two of the physical security guidelines recommended by Cisco.

Question 6

What does the acronym AAA stand for? What does each word mean to network security?

Question 5 Answer

Cisco recommends the following physical security guidelines:

- Deploy adequate physical access controls.
- To the extent possible, ensure that physical access cannot comprise other security measures.
- Ensure that you can recover easily in the event of device theft.
- Be sure to use cryptography for data that travels on equipment or networks that are out of your control.

Question 6 Answer

AAA stands for

- **Authentication**—Verifying a network user's identity
- **Authorization**—Verifying that the user is permitted to do what they are trying to do
- **Accounting**—Auditing access of recourses for security and billing purposes

Question 7

Name at least five ways a user can authenticate himself on a computer network.

Question 8

Name at least two authentication guidelines that are recommended by Cisco.

Question 7 Answer

There are many ways for authentication to function. The following can be used:

- Username/password
- Personal identification number (PIN)
- Private cryptographic key
- Password token card
- Smartcard
- Hardware key
- Fingerprint
- Retina pattern
- Voice
- Face recognition

Question 8 Answer

Cisco Systems recommends the following:

- Use strong authentication on users from external networks.
- Use strongest authentication mechanism when the most valuable resources are being accessed.
- Make authentication mechanisms user-friendly.
- Integrate authentication with existing user databases.

Question 9

Name at least one Cisco recommendation when it comes to network authorization.

Question 10

Name at least one guideline that Cisco recommends for the transmission of confidential data.

Question 9 Answer

Cisco recommends the following when it comes to authorization on the network:

- **Use the principle of least privilege**—Each user should use an account that gives him just enough privileges to accomplish what he needs, and no more.

- **Use the principle of defense in depth for valuable resources**—Each security mechanism should back up others.

- Never trust client-supplied settings.

Question 10 Answer

These guidelines include the following:

- Carefully evaluate locations in which confidentiality is necessary.

- Use strongest cryptography possible.

- Use well known and strong cryptography algorithms.

- Do not merely focus on confidentiality.

Question 11

The Internet Connectivity Module often features a DMZ. What is a DMZ?

Question 12

What is spoofing in network security?

Question 11 Answer

A demilitarized zone (DMZ) network contains a host that has been compromised. A DMZ is typically created using two firewalls, and it permits public access for select services.

Question 12 Answer

Spoofing means that the client is falsifying its true identity. IP address spoofing is a common method for gaining access to secured networks.

Section 14

Voice

An exciting area of networking technology involves the packetizing of voice and the transmission of these packets across the data network. This allows organizations to save on toll charges for Telco and eliminate expenses related to traditional PBX maintenance. This section ensures your readiness to answer questions about voice technologies and basic voice design concepts.

Question 1

Name at least two differences between a PBX and a PSTN switch.

Question 2

There are several types of trunks in a traditional voice network. What is the purpose of a tie trunk?

Question 1 Answer

There are several differences, including the following:

- PBXs are located in corporations, while PSTN switches are located in the public sector.
- PBXs do not feature the scalability of PSTN switches.
- PBXs tend to use proprietary protocols versus PSTN switches' open standards.
- PBXs connect telephones and other PBXs.

Question 2 Answer

Tie trunks connect traditional PBXs in a traditional voice network.

Question 3

What is the purpose of a FXS interface?

Voice

Question 4

What is QSIG?

Voice

Question 3 Answer

An FXS interface typically terminates at an analog telephone or fax machine.

Question 4 Answer

QSIG is a standards based protocol for use between PBXs. QSIG does not place any restrictions on private numbering plans.

Question 5

According to the open standard for converged networks, what are the three independent layers of the packet-switching model?

Question 6

Name at least three benefits of the H.323 protocol.

Question 5 Answer

The three layers of the model are as follows:

- Packet Infrastructure layer
- Call Control layer
- Open Service Application layer

Question 6 Answer

The H.323 protocol features the following benefits:

- Establishes standards for compression and decompression
- Provides for interoperability
- Provides network independence
- Permits platform and application independence
- Permits bandwidth management
- Supports multicast
- Enhanced flexibility

Question 7

Name at least three components of H.323.

Question 8

A key component of the Cisco IP telephony implementation is the replacement of the traditional PBX. Which Cisco component does this?

Question 7 Answer

The possible components are

- Terminals
- Gateways
- Gatekeepers
- MCUs

Question 8 Answer

Cisco CallManager

Question 9

What mechanism allows you to associate
destination phone numbers with IP addresses?

Question 10

Variation in the delay of received packets is
referred to as what?

Question 9 Answer

Dial peers

Question 10 Answer

Jitter

Question 11

What is a common benchmark used to determine the quality of sound?

Voice

Question 12

Which new voice technology is connection-oriented, uses small, fixed-sized cells, and supports different classes of service?

Voice

Question 11 Answer

Mean Opinion Score (MOS), which is a common, subjective benchmark for quantifying the performance of the speech codec. Sound quality, on the other hand, is called fidelity.

Question 12 Answer

Voice Over ATM (VoATM)

Question 13

Name one of the three typical sources of fixed delay in a network.

Voice

Question 14

Bandwidth availability is one of the biggest challenges with VoIP. Which technology attempts to assist this by focusing on packets of silence?

Voice

Question 13 Answer

Sources of delay include

- Propagation delay
- Serialization delay
- Processing delay

Question 14 Answer

Voice Activity Detection suppresses packets of silence.

Question 15

Which QoS congestion management mechanism features fair queuing with guaranteed bandwidth based on defined classes and weights, with a strict priority queue for voice traffic?

Voice

Question 16

What is defined as the probability that calls will be blocked while attempting to seize circuits?

Voice

Question 15 Answer

Low latency queuing (LLQ)

Question 16 Answer

Grade of service (GoS)

Question 17

What is a hardware component on a voice gateway that converts voice signal information to packet-based protocols?

Voice

Question 18

What mechanism helps to keep excess voice traffic off of the data network?

Voice

Question 17 Answer

Digital Signal Processor (DSP)

Question 18 Answer

Call Admission Control (CAC)

Section 15

Network Management

When network management is designed into the
network properly, it can save the organization massive
amounts of time and money. This section ensures that
you are prepared for difficult CCDA exam questions
about network management issues and solutions.

Question 1

Within the set of technologies referred to as SNMP, what component collects and stores information, responds to managers' request for information, and handles the generation of traps?

Question 2

Many types of SNMP messages circulate in a network management system. Which message type is an unsolicited alarm to a manager?

Question 1 Answer

The SNMP agent performs these functions.

Question 2 Answer

An SNMP trap message is an unsolicited alarm to a manager.

Question 3

What is the much-awaited enhancement to SNMP v3?

Question 4

Within the set of technologies referred to as SNMP, which component is a collection of managed objects, each of which possesses a unique identifier?

Question 3 Answer

SNMP v3 is to feature much awaited security enhancements.

Question 4 Answer

A management information base (MIB).

Question 5

What major enhancement does RMON2 present?

Question 6

At what layer of the OSI model does CDP operate?

Question 5 Answer

RMON2 allows visibility into all layers of the OSI model, as opposed to the Layer 1 and 2 monitoring of which RMON1 is capable.

Question 6 Answer

CDP operates at Layer 2.

Question 7

Name at least four items you can learn by using CDP.

Question 8

NetFlow can be used for network planning and user and application monitoring. For what other purposes can NetFlow be used?

Question 7 Answer

You can learn the following items by using CDP:

- Device ID
- Local interface
- Hold time
- Capability
- Platform
- Port ID
- Address

Question 8 Answer

NetFlow can also be used for accounting and billing purposes.

Question 9

Syslog messages each have a level. What is the level for emergency messages, and what is the level for debugging messages?

Network Management

Question 10

What does the ISO define as the five functional areas of network management?

Network Management

Question 9 Answer

Emergency messages have a level of 0. Debugging messages have a level of 7.

Question 10 Answer

The five functional areas are as follows:

- Fault management
- Configuration management
- Accounting management
- Performance management
- Security management

Question 11

Which Cisco network management product focuses on configuration, performance, and fault management, and is web-based for user-friendliness?

Network
Management

Question 12

Internetwork Performance Monitor (IPM) relies on what built-in intelligence of Cisco routers?

Network
Management

Question 11 Answer

CiscoWorks

Question 12 Answer

IPM relies on the Service Assurance Agent (SAA), which is built into most routers.

CCDA-DESGN Quick Reference Sheets

Network Design Methodologies

PDIOO

PDIOO is an excellent reflection of a modern network's life cycle. It stands for the following:

- Planning
- Design
- Implementation
- Operation
- Optimization

Although design exists as one of the steps, some design elements must be considered for all the steps.

Note While retirement is not part of the official steps of PDIOO, it is a legitimate fact of the network life cycle. Equipment is consistently taken out of production because of its age.

Design Methodology

The design methodology can be derived from PDIOO and is closely related. It consists of the following eight steps:

1. Identify customer requirements.
2. Characterize the existing network.
3. Design the topology and network solutions.
4. Plan the implementation.
5. Build a pilot.
6. Document the design.
7. Implement and verify.
8. Monitor and redesign.

Note Many people view the building of a pilot as an optional step.

ROI

The network designer should always consider the client's return on investment (ROI) when implementing any design approach. ROI is a measure of the financial savings or increase in revenues that will result from the implementation of a specific technology.

Top-Down Design Approach

Using the top-down approach, you first examine the organization's needs (for example, Voice over IP [VoIP]), and then you suggest technologies based on these needs. The network's physical implementations are derived from the requirements. Top-down design guidelines include the following:

- Careful analysis of customer requirements.
- Use the Open System Interconnection (OSI) model as a guide.
- Gather additional data about the network.

Although the top-down approach is more time-consuming than other approaches, its advantages include the following:

- Involves meeting customer requirements
- Provides clients with a straightforward "picture" of the network
- Typically meets the client's current and future requirements

Bottom-Up Design Approach

With the bottom-up approach, the network devices are selected first. This approach is typically used when there is little time for the design, which must be accomplished quickly. This design approach often leads to a required re-design at some future date.

Decision Tables

You need to consider using decision tables to assist with your design engagements. These tables assist you in making systematic decisions when multiple options exist in the design. When designing networks, you can use decision tables to determine which routing protocols, types of security, and physical topologies to implement, to name a few.

The following guidelines exist for creating decision tables:

- Decide where the use of decision tables is appropriate and required.
- Gather all possible options.
- Create a table of requirements and options.

- Match requirements with options.
- Select the option that has the most matches.

Evaluating Organizational Policies and Procedures

Network Organization Models

Classically, models were built on the concept of *vertical integration*. With this model, almost all production came from the internal organization. Today's internetworks promote models based on *horizontal integration*. Horizontal integration allows the business to form many partnerships with other businesses and share information for the good of each organization.

The modern *ecosystem model*, made possible by modern networking technologies, permits a tight integration of employees, customers, partners, and suppliers. This ecosystem model calls upon horizontal integration wherever necessary for the achievement of business objectives.

Network Organizational Architecture Components

Layered architecture that includes the following:

- Applications
- Enabling network solutions
- Prerequisite systems
- Network infrastructure, including intelligent network services (content networking, storage networking, VoIP)

Organizational Policies

Polices are used to achieve organizational goals:

- Common legal and regulatory policies
- Organizationally specific polices; examples include technology preferences, vendor preferences, and employment policies

Policies vary over time in a policy cycle.

Organizational Procedures

Organizational procedures stem from an organizational structure that typically includes various departments, such as marketing, finance, and engineering.

The network designer should scrutinize the information flows that move between these departments.

The network should contribute to all the organizational goals by adhering to the following:

- Functionality
- Scalability
- Availability
- Performance
- Manageability
- Efficiency

Examining Customer Requirements

Scope

Questions to ask include the following:

- New design or redesign?
- Is the design for a segment, a subset, or the entire network?
- Does the design address a single function or full functionality?
- What layers of the OSI model are involved in the design?

Design Data-Gathering Steps

Step 1 Determine organizational goals.

Step 2 Examine all organizational constraints (budget, personnel, policies, and scheduling).

Step 3 Examine planned applications and network services (security, QoS, management, high availability, and IP multicast).

Step 4 Determine technical goals (improve performance, improve security, improve reliability, decrease downtime, modernize technologies, improve scalability, and simplify management).

Step 5 Examine technical constraints (existing equipment, bandwidth availability, application compatibility, and personnel qualifications).

Characterizing the Existing Network

The following are general steps to characterizing the existing network:

Step 1 Collect input from network customers.

—Network topology

—Network services

—Network solutions and applications

—Expected network functionality

—Identify network modules

Step 2   Perform network audit.

Step 3   Perform traffic analysis.

Network Auditing

Provides details that were not gathered during initial data collection, including the following:

• Hardware/software specifics

• Configurations

• Usage data

Network Auditing Recommendations

• Leverage existing auditing tools.

• Introduce additional tools as needed.

• Minor changes to the network might be necessary to collect the required data; log these changes and reverse when complete.

• Automated auditing approaches should be employed in large networks.

• Create summary reports based on detailed information.

Manual Network Auditing Tools

• Monitoring commands on devices:

—Routers—Show tech-support; show processes cpu; show processes memory

—Switches—Show version; show running-config; show tech-support

—PIX—Show version; write terminal

• Scripting tools to collect information in large networks

Automated Network Auditing Tools

• CiscoWorks

• Cisco Secure Scanner

• Third party: HP OpenView, Visio, Tivoli, and so on

Network Traffic Analysis

• Cisco IOS manual analysis

—NBAR

—NetFlow

• Cisco analysis products

—FlowCollector; Network Data Analyzer

• Third party

—Sniffer; Network Monitor; EtherPeek; MRTG

Summary Report

This document summarizes the results of characterizing the existing network. It should do the following:

• Describe the required software features.

• Describe possible problems.

• Identify actions necessary for modifying the network.

• Influence the customer regarding requirements and changes.

Implementing the Design Methodology

You must document the design implementation in as many steps as possible. Remember the following recommendations:

• If there are multiple complex implementation steps, implement each separately (advantages include easier rollback and troubleshooting reduction).

• If there are not multiple complex steps, proceed with the implementation as an entirety.

The implementation should consist of phases, which should each consist of steps. Each step should contain the following elements:

• Description

• Reference to appropriate design documents

• Detailed implementation guidelines

• Detailed rollback guidelines

• Estimated time required for implementation

Pilot Versus Prototype

Pilots and prototypes can be used to test designs after the documentation phases and are often referred to as proofs of concept:

• Pilot network—Tests and verifies the design before the network is launched

• Prototype network—Tests and verifies a redesign in an isolated network before applying it to the existing network

Failure of the pilot or prototype might warrant redesigns.

Documenting the Design

The final design document should contain elements such as the following:

- Introduction
- Design requirements
- Existing network infrastructure
- Design
- Proof of concept
- Implementation plan
- Appendices

Network Hierarchies

Because of the complexity of modern networks and the critical nature these networks play in today's organizations hierarchical designs are necessary.

The Cisco classic hierarchical network model consists of the following three layers:

- **Access layer**—Used to provide access to the network for network users; security (especially authentication) is important at this layer to verify that the user should access the network; L2 switching is typically used in conjunction with VLANs; L3 switching can be used to connect remote offices.

- **Distribution layer**—Allows users to access resources that are not local to them; often referred to as policy-based connectivity because quality of service (QoS) mechanisms are often used; media translations are often performed at this layer; L3 switching is performed here.

- **Core layer**—High-speed transfer of information through the network; fault-tolerance is often performed here to guarantee connectivity through the network; L2 or L3 switching is implemented in the core.

Three Layer Hierarchical Network Model

Modular Network Designs

The three-layer network hierarchical network model is too simplistic. Instead, a new, more sophisticated model is needed.

Enterprise Composite Network Model

The network hierarchical model can still be used within the Enterprise Composite Network model; it can exist in any of the modules, as needed.

Enterprise Composite Network Model

Enterprise Campus	Enterprise Edge	Service Provider Edge
Management Module	E-Commerce Module	ISP Modules
Building Access Module	Internet Connectivity Module	Public Switched Telephone Network (PSTN) Module
Building Distribution Module	Remote Access/VPN Module	Frame Relay/ATM/PPP Module
Campus Backbone Module	WAN Module	
Server Farm Module		
Edge Distribution Module		

The Enterprise Composite Network model consists of the following three main functional areas:

- **Enterprise campus**—Contains modules that build a robust campus network.
- **Enterprise Edge**—Contains elements that are required to secure communications from the Campus to remote partners, mobile users, and the Internet.
- **Service Provider Edge**—These modules enable communication with WAN technologies and ISPs.

The Enterprise campus area consists of the following modules:

- **Campus Infrastructure**—Contains the building access, building distribution, and campus backbone submodules; notice the relation to the network hierarchical model.

Campus Infrastructure Module

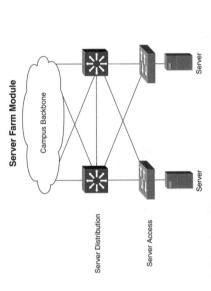

Campus Backbone

Building Distribution

Building Access

- **Network management**—Includes intrusion detection, system logging, TACACS+/ RADIUS authentication, network monitoring, and general configuration management.
- **Server farm**—Key servers that provide services such as e-mail, database, and DNS for end users.
- **Edge distribution**—Aggregates connectivity from the various elements in the Enterprise Edge area and routes traffic into the campus backbone.

Server Farm Module

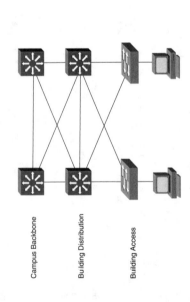

Campus Backbone

Server Distribution

Server Access

Server

Server

The Enterprise Edge functional area consists of the following modules:

- **E-commerce**—Consists of all elements needed to provide a robust e-commerce solution—including web servers, application servers, database servers, and fire-walls.
- **Internet connectivity**—Provides users with Internet access; includes SMTP, DNS, FTP, and HTTP servers.
- **Remote access and VPN**—Provides remote access to the network over secure VPN connections; includes dialin concentrators, VPN concentrators, firewalls, and Layer 2 switches.
- **WAN**—Contains the WAN technologies that connect different areas of the orga-nization, including remote offices and SOHO sites.

The Service Provider Edge functional area consists of the following three modules:

- **Internet service provider**—Enables the organization to access the Internet.
- **PSTN**—Provides dialup access for ISDN, analog, and wireless telephony.
- **Frame Relay/ATM**—Contains all WAN technologies that provide permanent connectivity with remote sites of the organization.

Switching Design Considerations

You must consider the following important design factors:

- Geography
- Applications
- Physical cabling
- Data link layer (shared or switched)
- Type of traffic forwarding (L2 or L3)

Table 1   Copper Versus Fiber

	Copper	Fiber
Bandwidth	Ethernet: < 1 Gbps LRE: < 15 Mbps	< 50 Gbps
Range	Ethernet: < 100 m LRE: < 1.5 km	Multimode: < 550 m Single Mode: < 100 km
Deployment area	Wiring closet	Inter-building
Other Considerations	Interference	Potential for coupling misalignment
Installation Cost	Cheap	Expensive

Shared Versus Switched

Advantages of switched networks over shared include the following:

- Higher bandwidth support
- Larger network diameter possible
- Additional L2 and L3 services
- High availability

Network Application Comparison Criteria

The following are important network parameters that should be considered when analyzing the applications for the network:

- Connectivity type
- Required throughput
- High availability
- Total network cost

L2 and L3 Design Considerations

- What network services are required (QoS, and so forth)?
- What size are the network segments?
- What level of availability is required?

In general, L2 switches are not capable of intelligent load sharing, L3 switches do feature this capability.

Spanning Tree Protocol

The protocol with enhancements can cause problems of the to potential 50-second delay in convergence. Enhancements include the following:

- PortFast—Ports that are connected to end systems; these ports skip the listening and learning states; used on access layer switches.
- BPDU Guard—Helps to ensure that loops are not introduced with the PortFast feature; if BPDUs are received on a PortFast interface, the interface enters errdisable.
- BPDU Filtering—Eliminates the transmission of BPDUs.
- UplinkFast—Used on access layer devices to enable the quick failover to a redundant path to the root upon a directly connected link failure.
- BackboneFast—Must be enabled on all switches; allows for quicker failover in the event of an indirect failure of a link to the root.
- STP Loop Guard—STP loop inconsistent port state is used to help prevent loops in the network resulting from failed BPDU reception.
- BPDU Skew Detection—Allows for syslog messages to be generated because of late-arriving BPDUs.
- Unidirectional Link Detection—Helps to determine a link's proper physical status
- Rapid Spanning Tree—802.1W; enhanced version of Spanning Tree that adds the functionality found in the Cisco proprietary solutions of PortFast, UplinkFast, and BackboneFast.
- Multiple STP—802.1S; VLANs can be mapped to specific spanning tree instances.

Campus Design Details

When designing the campus modules such as the server farm, the backbone, and so on, it is important to consider factors such as the need for scalability and performance. Table 2 helps you consider such factors.

Table 2 Factors to Consider When Designing Campus Modules

	Access		Distribution	Backbone	Server Farm	Edge Distribution
L2 or L3	L2	L3	L3	L2/L3	L3	L3
Scalability	High		Med	Low	Med	Low
High Availability	High		Med	High	High	Med
Performance	Low		Med	High	High	Med
Cost per Port	Low		Med	High	High	Med

80/20 Rule

The 80/20 rule is the traffic flow rule of a traditional network. It features access to servers that are located in the workgroups with end users. As a result, 80 percent of the access stays in the local workgroup. Only 20 percent of the traffic must be routed out of the local workgroup.

20/80 Rule

This rule is observed in modern networks. With this traffic flow pattern, servers are located in remote server farms. This means that only 20 percent of the traffic stays within the local workgroup, while 80 percent of the traffic is destined for remote areas.

Multicast

Switches flood multicast traffic by default, just as they would broadcast traffic. Two mechanisms are commonly employed in Cisco networks to more efficiently deal with multicasts. These mechanisms are detailed here:

- **Cisco Group Management Protocol (CGMP)**—A Cisco proprietary solution that allows the router to communicate with the switch and inform the switch of the presence of group members off of certain ports.
- **IGMP snooping**—The switch examines multicast receiver registrations and forwards traffic based on this information.

QoS

QoS is the process of managing the following in the campus network:

- Delay
- Variable delay (jitter)
- Packet drop
- Bandwidth

QoS categories include the following:

- **Classification and marking**—Involves categorizing traffic into different classes to allow for specialized treatment of various types of traffic.
- **Scheduling**—Determining the order in which queues are to be serviced.
- **Congestion management**—Queuing techniques are used to ensure that priority traffic gets better treatment through the congested areas of the network.
- **Policing and shaping**—To control rates, traffic shaping stores frames in buffers; traffic policing drops or lowers the priority of frames.

Access Layer Considerations

The access layer module should focus on the following considerations:

- Number of ports required
- Physical layer cabling
- Performance required
- Redundancy required
- Speeds required
- VLANs and STP configuration
- Additional features (QoS, multicast, and so on)

Distribution Layer Considerations

The distribution layer model should focus on the following considerations:

- L2 or L3 switching
- Performance required
- Number of ports required
- Redundancy required
- Additional features
- Manageability required

Core Layer Considerations

The following considerations should be the focus of the core layer module:

- L2 or L3 switching
- Performance required
- Number of ports required
- Redundancy required

Single L2 VLAN Core Design

Advantages

- Simple to design and implement
- Requires single subnet
- No STP convergence issues

Disadvantages

- No broadcast/multicast controls
- L3 peering issues in the distribution layer

Split L2 Core Design

Advantages

- Two equal cost paths across the backbone for fast convergence and load sharing

Disadvantages

- No broadcast/multicast controls

L3 Core Design

Advantages

- Reduced L3 peering
- Flexible without STP loops
- Broadcast/multicast controls
- Scalable
- Intelligent network services present

Disadvantages

- Potential for performance degradation

Dual-Path L3 Core Design

Advantages

- Two equal-cost paths to every network destination
- Quick recovery from link failures
- Double-link capacity

Server Farm Module

The following issues must be addressed with the server farm module:

- Access controls must be in place to secure access.
- There tend to be massive traffic demands.
- Connectivity—Servers connected by a single NIC, a dual NIC, or a server load-balancing switch.

Edge Distribution Module

This module must protect the campus from the following occurrences:

- Unauthorized access
- IP spoofing
- Network reconnaissance
- Packet sniffers

Enterprise WAN Solutions

Traditional WAN Technologies

Traditional WAN technologies can be categorized as follows:

- Leased lines—Point-to-point; typically synchronous serial connections that are dedicated for the organization's use; expensive.
- Circuit switched—Asynchronous serial, ISDN; path between endpoints defined for the duration of the call only.

- **Packet switched**—Frame Relay, SMDS, PVCs, or SVCs used to deliver data between endpoints
  —Star topology
  —Fully meshed
  —Partial mesh
- **Cell switched**—ATM; fixed sized cells transmitted quickly through the WAN

Emerging Technologies

- **DSL**—High bandwidth over existing copper telephone lines
- **Long Reach Ethernet (LRE)**—Offers 15 Mbps across increased distances; relies on technologies from DSL
- **Cable**—High-speed connections that use a hybrid of coaxial cable and fiber optic media
- **Wireless**—Electromagnetic waves form the physical media

Application Drivers for WAN Selection

- Response Time
- Throughput
- Packet Loss
- Reliability

Table 3   Bandwidth

Technology	Approximate Bandwidth
Asynchronous dialup	56 Kbps
ISDN – BRI	128 Kbps
ISDN – PRI, Frame Relay	1.544 Mbps
ADSL	8 Mbps
LRE	15 Mbps
Cable	27 Mbps
Wireless	44 Mbps

Bandwidth Optimization Techniques

Bandwidth optimization techniques support the following compression options:

- FRF.9 Frame Relay Payload Compression
- STAC or Predictor
- HDLC
- X.25
- PPP using Predictor
- Van Jacobson TCP/IP Header Compression
- MPCC

It is more efficient to have special hardware handle compression versus having software enable compression.

Window Size

Window size refers to the maximum amount of data that can be transmitted before an acknowledgment is required.

Queuing Services

The hardware queue uses first-in, first-out (FIFO).

The software queue can use other methods:

- WFQ—Weighted fair queuing
- PQ—Priority queuing
- CQ—Custom queuing

Note   For details on traffic shaping versus policing, refer to the QoS in the section, "Campus Design Details."

WAN Backup Technologies

- Dial backup routing
- Permanent secondary WAN link
- Shadow PVC
- Dial backup
- Internet
  —Generic routing encapsulation (GRE)
  —IPSec

Based on a label that is placed on the data, multiprotocol label switching (MPLS) forwards IP packets. This allows for efficient transmission of information and still permits complex QoS:

- **Label Switched Routers (LSRs)**—Switching and routing packets on the basis of a label that has been appended to each packet
- **Forwarding Equivalence Class (FEC)**—Defined flows
- **Label Switched Path (LSP)**—A path through the network
- **Label stacking**—A labeled packet can carry many labels

IP Addressing

Addressing can be flat or hierarchical. IP addresses are hierarchical; MAC addresses are flat. IP addresses consist of host portion and network portion, in addition to the following:

- 32 bits long—4 octets
- Usually presented in dotted decimal

The subnet mask indicates where the network portion ends and where the host portion begins. Use the following formula to determine the number of hosts that are supported:

- $2^n - 2$, where n is the number of bits used

To determine the number of subnets, use the following formula:

- 2^n, where n is the number of bits used

Address Classes

- Class A—First octet starts with 0; 0 to 127
- Class B—First octet starts with 10; 128 to 191
- Class C—First octet starts with 110; 192 to 233
- Class D—First octet starts with 1110; 224 to 239
- Class E—First octet starts with 1111; 240 to 255

Conversion Table

The eight bits in an octet have the following decimal values:

1	1	1	1	1	1	1	1
128	64	32	16	8	4	2	1

Defining Subnets

Some bits from host portion used to define additional subnetworks.

Design Questions to Answer

- How large is the network?
- How many locations does the network have?
- What are the IP addressing requirements for the locations?
- What class and how many networks can be obtained from the public number authority?

Private IPv4 Addresses

The following addresses are reserved for private use and cannot be used on public network:

- 10.0.0.0/8
- 172.16.0.0/12
- 192.168.0.0/16

Network Address Translation

Allows for the translation of one private address to one public address, or many private addresses to one public address.

Route Summarization

Hierarchy can be implemented in the addressing plan, which allows for summarization and smaller routing tables.

Fixed Length Subnet Masking

Unfortunately, some dynamic routing protocols require fixed length subnet masking. This means that all subnets must have the same subnet mask, making for inefficient address use.

Variable Length Subnet Masking

Variable length subnet masking allows the use of different subnet mask lengths and makes for more efficient routing and increased use of summarization.

Classful Versus Classless Routing Protocols

- **Classful routing**—Subnet masks are not included in routing updates; FLSM is required.
- **Classless routing**—Subnet masks are included; VLSM is possible.

Assigning Addresses

- Static—Large amount of administrative overhead; can be prone to errors
- Dynamic—Easier to manage; DHCP
- Automatic—Automatic assignment of private IP address

Name Resolution

DNS is a naming service that uses one server or a system of servers to dynamically handle resolution.

IPv6

Advantages to the new system include the following:

- 128-bit address size from 32 bit; increases the address space dramatically
- No need for NAT
- Site multihoming—Sites might carry multiple IP prefixes
- Fixed header sizes for more efficient processing
- Improved privacy and security
- New capabilities for labeling traffic for QoS
- Increased mobility features
- Increased multicast features

IPv6 Address Formats

IPv6 address formats are a series of 16-bit fields written in hexadecimal and separated by colons. The following shortcuts exist:

- Leading zeros can be omitted.
- Two colons can represent successive fields of zeros; this is permitted once in an address.

IPv6 Header

IPv6 header consists of 40 octets, as follows:

- Version
- Traffic class
- Flow label
- Payload length
- Next header
- Hop limit

- Source address
- Destination address

IPv6 Address Types

No longer are there broadcast addresses; now, a several types of IPv6 addresses exist:

- Unicast—Single source to destination, as in IPv4
- Anycast—Used to send traffic to the nearest interface that possesses the anycast address
- Multicast—Used to send traffic to a set of interfaces that belong to a special multicast address group, as in IPv4
- Link-local address—A unicast address that is automatically configured on an interface; automatically permits local communication
- Site-local address—Similar to the current private IP address space
- Global aggregatable address—Allows for globally unique addressing and promotes the use of address aggregation

IPv6 Routing Protocols

Interior Gateway Protocols (IGPs)

- RIPng
- OSPF v3
- IS-IS

Exterior Gateway Protocol (EGP)

- BGP4+

IPv6 Address Assignment

Static

Dynamic

- Link-local
- Stateless—Done from router
- Stateful using DHCP v6

IPv4 to IPv6 Deployment

- Dual stack—System runs both IPv4 and IPv6.
- Tunneling—Encapsulates IPv6 packets into IPv4 packets, and vice versa.
- Translation—One protocol is translated into another to facilitate communications.

outing Protocols

Static Versus Dynamic

Static (manually) created routes do have their place, as shown by the following examples:

- Routing to and from a stub network
- Small networks
- Special features, such as dial-on-demand routing (DDR)
- Specifying routes for dialin environments

Distance Vector Versus Link-State

Distance Vector

- Examples include RIP v1, RIP v2, and IGRP (Interior Gateway Routing Protocol).
- Entire routing tables are transferred periodically between systems.
- Tend to converge slowly.
- Offer limited scalability.
- Easy to implement and maintain.

Link-State

- Examples include OSPF and IS-IS.
- Each router makes independent routing decisions based on local databases.
- Faster convergence.
- Better scalability.
- Feature less routing traffic overhead.
- Advertise updates that occur in the rather than flooding updates, like distance vector.
- Requires more knowledge and expertise to configure.

Hybrid

- An example is EIGRP.
- It has features of both distance vector and link state protocols.

Interior Versus Exterior

Interior Gateway Protocols (IGPs)

- Examples include OSPF, IS-IS, EIGRP, and RIP.
- These routing protocols handle the dynamic routing that occurs within private company networks.
- They feature fast convergence and easier configuration.

Exterior Gateway Protocols (EGPs)

- An example includes BGP.
- They handle routing between autonomous systems.
- They feature slower convergence and require more complex configurations.

Routing Protocols Metrics

- RIP—Hop count
- IGRP—Bandwidth, delay
- EIGRP—Bandwidth, delay
- BGP—AS-PATH
- OSPF—Cost (bandwidth)
- IS-IS—Link metrics (default)

Routing Protocol Convergence

- RIP—Hold-down + 1 or 2 update intervals
- IGRP—Hold-down + 1 or 2 update intervals
- EIGRP—Seconds
- OSPF—Seconds

Hierarchical Versus Flat

Flat Routing Protocols

- Examples are classful routing protocols.
- Propagate routing information throughout the entire network.
- They are not scalable.

Hierarchical Routing Protocols

- Examples are classless.
- Divide the network into areas; they do not propagate information throughout the entire network—areas are used instead.
- They are scalable.

ODR Routing

Hub routers can dynamically maintain routes to stub network routers. Thanks to ODR (Cisco proprietary), there is not the overhead with a full-fledged dynamic routing protocol; this is ideal for hub and spoke topologies. ODR relies upon the Cisco Discovery Protocol (CDP).

RIP v2

RIPv2 is a classless version of RIP (VLSM supported). It uses multicast rather than broadcast to propagate routing information. However, the hop count limitation is still 15.

EIGRP

A hybrid routing protocol, EIGRP uses the same metric as IGRP, but multiplies it by 256 to allow for greater flexibility. EIGRP is classless (supports VLSM). EIGRP uses the diffusing update algorithm (DUAL) to maintain fast convergence.

OSPF

OSPF is an extremely scalable link state routing protocol that also features excellent convergence. OSPF uses a cost metric that is based on bandwidth.

Integrated IS-IS

Integrated IS-IS supports OSI and IP networks and can do so simultaneously. Simple area design presents advantages over OSPF.

BGP

BGP is exterior routing protocol that is used to route on the Internet. It is a distance vector with many enhancements and allows administrators to heavily influence routing decisions to permit "strategic routing policies." BGP consists of iBGP, which is used for conveying routing information between routers within an AS. eBGP is used to move information between routers in different ASs. BGP can work with an IGP to learn about routes within an AS.

Advanced Routing Protocol Features

* **Redistribution**—The ability to run multiple routing protocols in a network and share information between them; can be one-way or two-way redistribution.
* **Filtering**—Controlling the information that is shared in routing and in redistribution.
* **Summarization**—Allows for the reduction of routing tables; one larger one can represent many subnets.

Security

Cisco network security should provide the following:

* Data integrity
* Data confidentiality
* Data availability

Major threats include the following:

* **Integrity violations**—Change data without authorization
* **Confidentiality breaches**—Users read data that they should not be able to read

Denial of Service Attacks

Denial of service (DoS) attacks compromise the availability of data. They typically involve flooding a network system with bogus traffic.

Reconnaissance Attacks

Under a reconnaissance attack, the network is being searched or scanned for potential targets.

Traffic Attacks

These attacks occur when data flowing through a network is compromised.

Network Security Practices

* **Risk assessment**—Defines the potential threats that exist
* **Security policy**—Defines how risks are managed
* **Security design**—Implements the security policy

Physical Security

Physical security, which includes console access to routers and switches cannot be overlooked. Guidelines include the following:

* Include physical access controls.
* Determine whether breached physical access can effect other security controls.
* Be able to recover quickly from theft.
* Ensure that you protect communications over insecure networks that you do not own.

AAA

AAA should be used in a secure network:

* **Authentication**—Verify the identity of the user who wants to access network resources
* **Authorization**—What can the user do in the network
* **Accounting**—Monitoring the access to the network

SAFE Blueprint

The Cisco Security Architecture for Enterprise (SAFE) blueprint provides a modular approach to securing the network. It also provides best practices for network designers and implementers.

SAFE Guidelines for Securing the Internet Connectivity Module

- Firewalls, routers, and IDS should be used to prevent network mapping attacks.
  - To ensure that exposed hosts are not compromised, use firewalls to protect and IDS to detect.
  - To stop hosts from being attacked by compromised hosts, use a DMZ, firewalls, host hardening, LAN access control, and IDS for monitoring.
  - DoS attacks on links—QoS mechanisms; IDS.
  - DoS attacks on hosts—host hardening and firewalls.
  - Introduction of malicious code—use application filtering.

SAFE Guidelines for Securing the E-Commerce Module

- Exposed hosts and applications—Use firewalls, host hardening, secure programming, and IDS.
- Hosts attacked from other hosts—Host hardening, firewalls, and IDS.
- DoS attacks at hosts—DMZ, firewalls, IDS, and LAN access controls.

SAFE Guidelines for Securing the Remote Access and VPN Module

- Risk of identity spoofing—Strong authentication
- Confidentiality and integrity—Strong encryption
- Compromised clients and remote sites—Firewalls and virus scanning

SAFE Guidelines for Securing the WAN Module

- Confidentiality and integrity—Strong encryption
- WAN misconfiguration—WAN peer authentication

SAFE Guidelines for Securing the Network Management Module

- Administrator impersonation—Authentication
- Compromise of management protocols—Secure protocols
- Accidental/deliberate misconfiguration—Authorization
- Responsibility avoidance—Auditing
- Management host—Separate management networks, firewalls, and IDS

SAFE Guidelines for Securing the Server Farm Module

- Compromise of exposed hosts—Firewalls, host hardening, secure applications, and IDS
- Compromise other hosts from compromised hosts—Firewalls, IDS, and LAN access controls

Voice

For classic voice communications, voice analog signals are converted to digital for transmission and are then converted back to analog for delivery.

PBX

The PBX is a business telephone system that features the following characteristics:

- Used in private business environment.
- Scales to n * 1000 phones.
- Primarily digital technology.
- Uses 64 Kbps circuits.
- Proprietary protocols to control phones (with the exception of the new QSIG and DPNSS.)
- Provides connectivity for business phones and call hold, music on hold, voice mail, and so forth.
- Usually connects to the PSTN using T1/E1 digital circuits.
- Supports analog and digital phones; typically proprietary.
- Advantages include free calls within the PBX system, and a great use of the trunk to the PSTN for external calls only; also, company can control moves, voice mail, and so forth.
- One disadvantage is that the company must have trained personnel for PBX maintenance.

PSTN Switch

The following are characteristics of the PSTN switch, which is used to create the PSTN network and is located in central offices:

- Used in the PSTN
- Scales to $n * 100,000$ phones
- Mainly digital technology
- Uses 64 Kbps circuits
- Uses open standard protocols
- Interconnects with other PSTN switches and PBXs
- Deployed in a hierarchy; CO switches connect to tandem switches—tandem switches connect to other tandem switches

Telephone Infrastructure

The following list includes various telephone infrastructure components that exist to ensure that everything is connected:

- **Local loop**—Physical cabling between the CO and the home
- **Station line**—Physical cabling between the PBX and telephones
- **Tie trunk**—Used to connect PBXs with each other
- **CO trunk**—Used to connect CO switches and PBXs
- **PSTN switch trunk**—Used to connect CO switches
- **Foreign exchange trunks**
  - **Foreign exchange office**—Interface that allows connection to a PSTN CO or a Foreign Exchange Station.
  - **Foreign exchange station**—An interface that typically terminates at a standard analog telephone or fax.

Telephony Signaling

Different telephony signaling must be used in the following two broad areas:

- **Subscriber signaling**—Used between a PSTN switch and a subscriber
- **Trunk signaling**—Between PSTN switches, between a PSTN switch and a PBX, or between PBX switches

There are four basic categories of signaling:

- **Supervision signaling**—Used to initiate telephone call requests and release calls, in addition to other functions
- **Address signaling**—Used to pass dialed digits to a PBX or PSTN switch
- **Call progress signals**—Used to indicate certain events such as a busy signal or an incoming call
- **Network management signals**—Used to control the assignment of circuits or to respond to overloads

Analog Signaling

- **Loop start**—Simplest form; used for most residences; not used for business because of "glare" (endpoints obtaining line simultaneously)
- **Ground start**—Uses positive recognition of connects and disconnects; not susceptible to glare; often used in the PBX loop
- **E&M (Receive and Transmit or Ear and Mouth)**—Signaling technique often used between PBXs

Analog and Digital Trunk Signaling

Analog signaling occurs through current flow in electrical circuits.

Digital signaling

- **Channel Associated Signaling (CAS)**—Not efficient and, therefore, is being abandoned; call setup signal is sent on the same channel as the voice call; examples include T1 using R1 signaling and DTMF.
- **Common Channel Signaling (CSS)**—A separate channel is used for call setup; examples include E1, ISDN, DPNSS, QSIG, and SS7.

ISDN

- PRI—23B+D
- BRI—2B + D

QSIG

QSIG is a standards-based protocol for inter-PBX communications.

Signaling System 7

Signaling System 7 (SS7) is signaling used within the PSTN; it is done on a separate data network.

Voice addressing is done to conform to ITU-T E.164; it is an international hierarchical system based on number codes. The North American Numbering Plan (NANP) is NXX-NXX-XXXX.

PSTN Services

- **Centrex**—Outsourced voice solution so the company does not need a PBX.
- **Virtual private voice networks**—Multiple PBXs that the corporation owns are connected by the PSTN.
- **Voice mail**
- **Call center**—Automatic Call Distribution is used to distribute calls to employees.
- **Interactive voice response**—Information exchanged with no employee intervention using touch-tones or voice responses.

VoIP

Why do we need VoIP? Here's why:

- PSTN is being overwhelmed with data, and it does a poor job with data.
- PSTN is too slow to deploy new features.
- Cost reduction.
- Packet-switched network can occur in three powerful layers: open-service application layer, call control layer, and packet infrastructure layer.
- Even with TDM, there can be low trunk efficiency.

H.323

H.323 is a standard for carrying video, audio, and data across the IP network as packets. It includes a set of standards—H.225 for call signaling and H.245 for media stream management—and uses four major components:

- **Terminals**—PCs with NetMeeting or IP telephones
- **Gateways**—Voice-enabled routers and switches
- **Gatekeepers**—Provides management of endpoints and establishment of calls; Cisco router or third party software
- **Multipoint Control Unit**—Endpoint on the LAN; can be on the terminal, gateway, or gatekeepers

Single-Site Design

Cisco CallManager, IP phones, and voice enabled router; gateway trunks are used to the PSTN for external calls.

Single-Site CCM Model

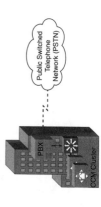

Centralized IP Telephony Design

Remote IP phones rely on a centralized Cisco CallManager. Again, the PSTN handles external calls.

Centralized Call-Processing CCM Model

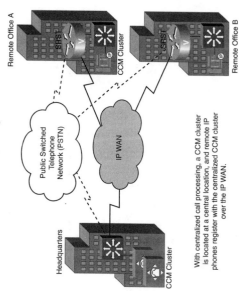

With centralized call processing, a CCM cluster is located at a central location, and remote IP phones register with the centralized CCM cluster over the IP WAN.

Internet IP Telephony Design

ISPs carry the voice traffic via the Internet; it is important that they support QoS.

Dial Plans

- **Voice ports**—Any port on the gateway that carries voice data; there are many interface types for this—ISDN PRI, FXS, FXO, ISDN BRI, T1-CAS.
- **Dial peers**—Associate physical voice ports with logical peers, including destination phone numbers with IP, Frame Relay, or ATM addresses. Four types include basic telephone service, VoIP, VoFR, and VoATM dial peers.
- **Call legs**—A logical connection between gateways.

Voice Issues

Delay—One way delay should be below 150 ms.

Types of delay include the following:

- Constant
  - Processing delay
  - Serialization delay
  - Propagation delay
- Variable
  - Queuing delay
  - Dejitter delay

Jitter —Variation in delay; dejitter buffer is used to combat this.

Packet Loss—Causes voice clipping; Cisco DSP can correct up to 30 ms of lost voice.

Echo—cho cancellation is used to combat this.

Coding and Compression Algorithms

Voice-Coding Standards

- PCM
- ADPCM
- LDCELP
- CS-ACELP
- CELP

- G.711
- G.726
- G.728

- G.729
- G.723.1

Mean Opinion Score

Mean Opinion Score (MOS) is a common, subjective benchmark for quantifying the performance of the speech codec. Sound quality, on the other hand, is called fidelity.

Call Control Functions

- H.225 call signaling channel
- H.245 control channel
- RAS signaling
- RTCP

VoFR

VoFR is not an end-to-end solution like VoIP. Intended to connect PBXs.

- Static FRF.11 trunks
- Dynamic switched VoFR calls

VoATM

VoATM are connection-oriented, small, fixed-size cells.

For variable bit rate (VBR), specify the following:

- Peak value
- Average value
- Burst value

QoS for Voice

Always grant strict priority for delay-sensitive traffic (voice) at the expense of other traffic types.

Congestion Management QoS Mechanisms

- **IP RTP priority**—Voice identified by RTP port numbers and classified into a priority queue
- **Priority queuing**—Uses four traffic queues
- **Custom queuing**—Sixteen queues that cycle round robin
- **Weighted fair queuing**—Divides bandwidth across queues based on weights
- **Class based weighted fair queuing**—Defined classes allow for bandwidth guarantees
- **Low latency queuing**—Fair queuing with guarantees and strict priority for voice

- On-Net—Private tie lines that are used whenever possible.
- Off-Net—Used when private tie lines are congested; called party not reachable on network; manual selection of off-net extension.

Grade of Service

Grade of service (GoS) is the probability of a call being blocked in the busiest hour.

Erlang Tables

Erlang tables combine offered traffic, the number of circuits, and GoS.

DSP

The DSP is a hardware component that allows the voice gateway module to transmit voice packets using IP on a data network.

Calculating Capacity for the WAN

- Number of simultaneous voice calls
- Sampling rate
- Codec
- Link type
- Header compression techniques
- VAD or no VAD

Call Admission Control

Call admission control (CAC) keeps excessive voice traffic off the network.

Campus IP Telephony Capacity Planning

- Cisco CallManager processing
- Network capacity and performance
- Trunking capacity

Network Management

SNMP

Simple Network Management Protocol (SNMP) forms the language of network management. It works with network management stations and agents, or devices that are monitored. MIBs store variables in the device that SNMP retrieves to obtain information about the device or configure the device.

SNMP Components

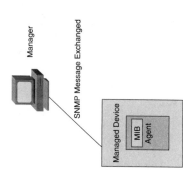

SNMP messages include the following:

- Get Request
- Get Next Request
- Set Request
- Set Next Request
- Trap

SNMP v 2 adds GetBulk and InformRequest, as well as data types with 64-bit values. SNMP v3 is not yet fully implemented yet; however, it is finally going to add much needed security mechanisms.

RMON

A method of self-collecting the information stored in MIBS regarding performance, RMON can set up performance thresholds and only generate traffic when these thresholds are exceeded. RMON1 views information through the data link layer, whereas RMON2 checks data through the seven layers of the OSI model.

CDP

Cisco Discovery Protocol (CDP) allows Cisco devices to discover the addresses and capabilities of directly connected neighbors. Many Cisco applications, such as Cisco-Works, rely on CDP:

- **NetFlow accounting**—Measures traffic flows moving through the device; can be used for accounting and billing, network planning, and user and application monitoring

Syslog

The router or switch automatically generates status and other messages; various levels indicate severity. It is best to send syslog messages to a syslog server, such as a UNIX or CiscoWorks box. A remote collector can even be used if the load is too much in a larger network.

FCAPS

The following are the five functional areas of network management, as defined by the ISO:

- Fault management
- Configuration management
- Accounting management
- Performance management
- Security management

Service Level Agreements

A service level agreement (SLA), or several of them, helps make up a service level contract. Common SLA metrics include the following:

- Availability
- Network delay
- Packet loss
- Network delay variation (jitter)

Service Level Management

Cisco Systems wants to provide end-to-end visibility of all aspects of service level management.

SLM planning steps include the following:

- Topology
  - Critical services
  - Usage of services
  - Responsibility of services
  - Acceptable response times

CiscoWorks

CiscoWorks is a suite of web-based applications for comprehensive network management. It focuses on FCAPS.

CiscoWorks — CD One

- Cisco View
- CiscoWorks Management Server
- Integration Utility

CiscoWorks — LAN Management Solutions (LMS)

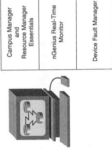

- Campus Manager and Resource Manager Essentials
- nGenius Real-Time Monitor
- Device Fault Manager

CiscoWorks — Routed WAN (RWAN) Solutions

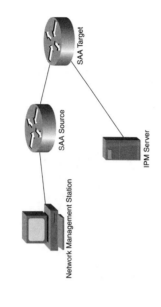

Access Control List Manager and Resource Manager Essentials

Internetwork Performance Monitor (IPM)

Service Assurance Agent

Embedded in router IOS; offers threshold violation notifications, scheduling, storage of historical information, and the ability to monitor per-class traffic.

Internetwork Performance Monitor

Exploits the SAA that is embedded in devices monitor and collects historical and real-time data about service levels.

IPM

SAA Target

SAA Source

Network Management Station

IPM Server

Part II

CCDP-ARCH

Section 1
Network Architectures

Section 2
The Enterprise Edge

Section 3
Network Management

Section 4
High Availability

Section 5
Network Security

Section 6
Quality of Service

Section 7
IP Multicasting

Section 8
VPNs

Section 9
Wireless LANs

Section 10
IP Telephony

Section 11
Content Networking

Section 12
Storage Networking

CCDP-ARCH Quick Reference Sheets

Section 1
Network Architectures

With the myriad of requirements for today's networks, the design process requires a robust modular framework that network designers can leverage. For years, the Cisco three-layer hierarchical design model (i.e., access, distribution, and core layers) was sufficient. However, e-commerce, security, virtual private networks (VPNs), and other emerging technologies require a more modern approach. Fortunately, Cisco developed a far more comprehensive model: the Enterprise Composite Network Model.

The flash cards in this section review the components of the Enterprise Composite Network Model and include step-by-step design processes for designing the Enterprise campus and the Server Farm modules. They also require you to make appropriate design decisions given a set of criteria. For example, you should be able to identify where technologies such as FastEthernet and Gigabit Ethernet are most applicable in a design.

Question 1

Identify the three primary key components of the Cisco AVVID framework.

Question 2

List at least two benefits provided by the Cisco AVVID framework.

Question 1 Answer

The Cisco Architecture for Voice, Video, and Integrated Data (AVVID) is an umbrella of technologies that allow a wide spectrum of technologies to be integrated into the same design framework. The primary components of AVVID include the following:

Network infrastructure—The hardware, software, and cabling that comprise the physical network.

Network services—Adds intelligence to the network by providing such features as network management, high availability, security, quality of service, and IP multicast.

Network solutions—Leverages the underlying network services and network infrastructure to provide solutions (such as IP telephony, content networking, and storage networking) for the end user.

Question 2 Answer

The Cisco comprehensive AVVID framework offers the following benefits:

- Integration
- Intelligence
- Innovation
- Interoperability

Question 3

When a designer selects components to meet design requirements, what are the three primary design concerns?

Network Architectures

Question 4

List the components of the Cisco traditional, three-layer hierarchical model.

Network Architectures

Question 3 Answer

Whether you are selecting, for example, a network management solution, a Layer 3 switch, or a firewall, the primary design concerns are the following:

- **Performance**—Measured in terms of responsiveness, throughput, and utilization.

- **Scalability**—A network's ability to rapidly expand its topology, addressing, and routing protocols.

- **Availability**—The measure of a device's or a network's uptime.

Question 4 Answer

In the early 1990s, Cisco introduced its three-layer hierarchical deign model. The three layers were

- **Access layer**—Provided workgroup access

- **Distribution layer**—Aggregated access layer devices and applied policies to traffic flows

- **Core layer**—Provided high-speed transport across the network backbone

Question 5

Describe the Enterprise campus functional area in the Enterprise Network Composite Model.

Network Architectures

Question 6

Identify the four modules in the Enterprise Edge functional area of the Enterprise Network Composite Model.

Network Architectures

Question 5 Answer

The Enterprise Network Composite Model includes three functional areas: Enterprise campus, Enterprise Edge, and Service Provider Edge. The Enterprise campus functional area is comprised of the following modules, which are used for campus networks:

- Campus infrastructure

- Network management

- Server farm

- Edge distribution

Question 6 Answer

The Enterprise Edge functional area sits between the Enterprise campus and the Service Provider Edge and contains the following modules:

- E-commerce

- Internet connectivity

- Remote access and VPN

- WAN

Question 7

Describe the purpose of the e-commerce
module.

Question 8

In which Enterprise Edge module would a DNS
server be categorized?

Question 7 Answer

The e-commerce module houses the servers that support a company's web-based transaction applications. These servers might include web, application, database, and security servers.

Question 8 Answer

The Enterprise Edge functional area is made up of the e-commerce, Internet connectivity, remote access/VPN, and WAN modules. For Internet users to access corporate resources by name, the corporate network requires a DNS server, which is therefore classified in the Internet connectivity module.

Question 9

In the Enterprise Composite Network Model, what is the purpose of the WAN module?

Question 10

Identify the Enterprise Edge module that contains dial-in access concentrators.

Question 9 Answer

The WAN module, which is one of the four Enterprise Edge modules, provides connectivity between a central site and remote sites. For example, a company might have a headquarters site and three remote sales office sites. If those remote sites connect back to the headquarters via WAN technologies (such as PPP, ATM, or Frame Relay), they are connecting to the WAN module.

Question 10 Answer

The remote access and VPN module of the Enterprise Edge module allow remote users and remote sites to connect back to a central site. One option for remote access is to allow users to dial directly into the central site via a modem. Therefore, the dial-in access concentrator is categorized as part of the remote access and VPN module.

Question 11

Describe the Service Provider Edge functional area of the Enterprise Composite Network Model.

Network Architectures

Question 12

Under which functional area of the Enterprise Composite Network Model would the PSTN be classified?

Network Architectures

Question 11 Answer

The Service Provider Edge allows the Enterprise campus to communicate with remote locations via services provided by the service providers that make up the Service Provider Edge. Components of the Service Provider Edge include the following:

- **Internet service provider (ISP)**—For connecting to the Internet

- **Public switched telephone network (PSTN)**—For connecting via the public telephone system

- **FR/ATM/PPP**—For interconnecting remote locations directly, via leased lines, permanent virtual circuits, or switched virtual circuits.

Question 12 Answer

The Public Switched Telephone Network (PSTN) is the traditional telephony network that provides telephony service to your home. It can be used to allow remote users to access resources at a central site. However, you as a network designer do not design the PSTN because it is managed independently. In the context of enterprise network design, the PSTN is a service provider service that can be integrated into the network design. Therefore, the PSTN is classified under the Service Provider Edge functional area of the Enterprise Composite Network Model.

Question 13

List at least three requirements for an Enterprise campus network design.

Network Architectures

Question 14

Identify the second step in the Enterprise campus design methodology.

Network Architectures

Question 13 Answer

The Enterprise campus network must meet the following design requirements:

- Functionality
- Performance
- Scalability
- Availability
- Manageability
- Cost effectiveness

Question 14 Answer

Designing the logical network topology is the second step in the Enterprise campus design methodology. The following seven steps are presented in the ARCH course for the Enterprise campus design methodology:

1 Identify requirements of existing enterprise applications and data flows.

2 Design the logical network topology (for example, identify VLANs).

3 Design the physical network topology (for example, identify Layer 1 through 3 components and technologies).

4 Identify Cisco devices that meet the previous criteria and diagram the network topology.

5 Select an appropriate IP addressing scheme.

6 Choose routing protocols.

7 Design the Edge Distribution module, which connects the Enterprise campus to the Enterprise Edge.

Question 15

As part of the first step to designing the Enterprise campus, you need to characterize existing applications. Identify at least three application characteristics that you might identify in this step.

Question 16

Describe the purpose of VLANs and list at least two ways in which VLANs can be defined (for example, what determines the devices grouped within a VLAN).

Question 15 Answer

While characterizing applications, typical application characteristics that you could identify include the following:

- Location of application
- Name of application
- Type of application
- Number of users
- Number of servers
- Bandwidth/delay tolerance/loss characteristics

Question 16 Answer

VLANs are broadcast domains that segment traffic. VLANs are often defined based on departmental or organizational boundaries; however, they can be defined based on geographical location. Another common approach to defining VLANs is to create VLANs for specific applications (such as voice, video, and data).

Question 17

Describe why campus-wide VLANs should not be used in a design.

Network Architectures

Question 18

Arrange the following transmission media types from least expensive to most expensive: multimode fiber, twisted pair, and single-mode fiber.

Network Architectures

Question 17 Answer

Having large, campus-wide VLANs can slow the convergence of the Spanning Tree Protocol (STP). For example, if the diameter (or the maximum number of switch hops) of a VLAN was seven switches, the STP timers would have to be higher than it would if the diameter was three switches.

If a problem occurs within a VLAN (such as a broadcast storm), the problem can be propagated over a larger area with a campus-wide VLAN. Also, campus-wide VLANs often need to support over-lapping STP domains, which can make troubleshooting more difficult.

Question 18 Answer

1 Twisted pair

2 Multimode fiber

3 Single-mode fiber

Of the transmission types listed, twisted pair, which uses copper, is the least expensive. Multimode fiber, which uses glass, is moderately expensive. Single-mode fiber, which also uses glass, must be manufactured to more exacting tolerances than multimode fiber. Specifically, single-mode fiber has to have a core diameter that is only large enough to allow the propagation of one "mode" (or one path) of light. Therefore, single-mode fiber is more expensive than multimode fiber.

Question 19

Where would 10 Mbps Ethernet technology be used in the Enterprise campus network?

Network Architectures

Question 20

What is the maximum speed of LRE?

Network Architectures

Question 19 Answer

10/100 network interface cards (NICs) are currently about as inexpensive as 10 Mbps Ethernet cards. So, realistically, 10 Mbps Ethernet would not be used in a new design. However, if 10 Mbps Ethernet technology already exists in the network and you wanted to leverage that existing investment, 10 Mbps Ethernet would only be used in the Building Access module because of its bandwidth limitations.

Question 20 Answer

Long-Reach Ethernet (LRE) can be used in buildings with existing Category 1, 2, or 3 wiring. Speeds for LRE range from 5 Mbps to 15 Mbps (full duplex).

Question 21

List two Ethernet trunking protocols.

Question 22

You have a Layer 2 switch that contains ports that belong to two different VLANs. Describe how ports from one VLAN can communicate with ports in the other VLAN.

Question 21 Answer

Trunking protocols allow traffic from multiple VLANs to be carried over a single physical link. The Cisco proprietary trunking protocol is Inter-Switch Link (ISL). The IEEE defined another trunking protocol: IEEE 802.1Q. With its recent enhancements, the IEEE 802.1Q standard is gaining popularity over ISL.

Question 22 Answer

VLANs are broadcast domains. So, you can think of a VLAN as being its own subnet. Routing must occur to transport traffic from one subnet to another; therefore, you need a device that makes forwarding decisions based on Layer 3 information (such as a router or a Layer 3 switch). So, the Layer 2 switch described in this scenario needs an external router or Layer 3 switch to transport traffic from one VLAN to another.

Question 23

You design a network that only has one VLAN per building access switch. Which trunking protocol should you use between the building access switches and the building distribution switches?

Question 24

Is Layer 3 switching most appropriate in the building access module or in the building distribution module?

Question 23 Answer

Because each building access switch only has one VLAN, *there is no need to trunk* to the building distribution switch. An exception to this approach would be if you had a management VLAN that existed on each switch in addition to the VLAN used for user traffic. In that instance, you could select either IEEE 802.1Q or ISL as your trunking protocol to transport both user and management VLAN traffic between the building access and building distribution modules.

Question 24 Answer

Layer 3 switching is most appropriate in the building distribution module. The building access module is the location at which end-user devices connect. Therefore, a building access switch can have ports that belong to various VLANs, but Layer 3 switching is not appropriate.

The building distribution module is responsible for aggregating building access switches, routing between VLANs, and applying policies. Therefore, Layer 3 switching is most appropriate in the building distribution module. Layer 3 switching is also applicable for many campus backbone networks.

Question 25

Step four of the Enterprise campus design methodology is to select Cisco hardware and software to meet the criteria that was defined in the first three steps. What web-based tool does the Cisco website offer to aid in selecting the appropriate hardware?

Question 26

Step five of the Enterprise campus design methodology is to select an appropriate IP addressing scheme. Describe a scenario in which you would specify PAT in a network's IP addressing scheme.

Question 25 Answer

The Cisco Product Advisor is a web-based tool that aids in the selection of Cisco hardware to meet design criteria. The Product Advisor is located at this URL:

http://www.cisco.com/warp/public/779/smbiz/service/advisor/

Question 26 Answer

PAT allows multiple internal systems to use a single public IPv4 address by keeping track of Layer 4 port number information associated with each session. Therefore, PAT is useful for networks that require Internet connectivity but do not have any publicly accessible servers. Conversely, static NAT maps a single internal IP address to a unique external (or public) IP address.

Question 27

Identify two routing protocols that are appropriate for Frame Relay point-to-multipoint networks.

Question 28

Describe the purpose of server SLB in server farm design.

Question 27 Answer

EIGRP and OSPF are appropriate routing protocols to use on Frame Relay point-to-multipoint networks. RIP and IGRP are not appropriate because of their periodic flooding of route information and their slow time to converge. Also, IS-IS does not adapt well to NBMA point-to-multipoint networks.

Question 28 Answer

SLB allows multiple requests for the same content to be distributed across multiple servers, each housing the same content. SLB therefore contributes to a server farm module design's scalability.

Network Architectures

Question 29

What are the characteristics of a server distribution switch (for example, low-end, mid-range, high-end, Layer 2, or Layer 3) in the server farm module?

Network Architectures

Question 30

Identify at least one technology that you could add to a server farm module to increase performance and scalability within that module.

Question 29 Answer

In the server farm module, mid-range to high-end switches (such as a Catalyst 6500 series switch) are recommended. Also, because the server distribution switch might be responsible for server load balancing and content routing, the switches used in that module should be Layer 3 switches.

Question 30 Answer

The server farm module can be scaled to support additional devices by adding ports to existing modular switches. Using technologies such as *EtherChannel*, or using *higher-speed interfaces* potentially increase the server farm module's performance.

The Spanning Tree Protocol (STP) runs between the server access layer and the server distribution layer. Therefore, selecting optimal STP approaches can increase the server farm module's performance. Specifically, the *IEEE 802.1s Multi-Instance Spanning Tree* protocol allows you to define various STP instances and assign VLANs to one of the specified instances. This approach negates the requirement for each VLAN to run its own instance of STP, as is the case with Per-VLAN Spanning Tree.

Section 2

The Enterprise Edge

CCDP-ARCH

The Enterprise Edge provides connectivity between the Enterprise Campus and the outside world. Specifically, traffic flowing to and from the Internet must pass through the Enterprise Edge. Remote users or sites that connect back to the Enterprise Campus connect through the Enterprise Edge. Also, WAN connections from remote offices often terminate in the Enterprise Edge.

Also consider e-commerce servers. You want Internet users to securely enter your site and perform transactions. However, you do not want them to reach the Enterprise Campus network. Therefore, the Enterprise Edge serves as an ideal location for e-commerce servers.

The flash cards in this section review the modules that comprise the Enterprise Edge. They also require you to make appropriate design decisions given a set of criteria. For example, you should be able to select appropriate Layer 1 and Layer 2 technologies based on parameters such as cost and speed.

Question 1

Identify the final step in the Cisco eight-step process for Enterprise Edge design.

Question 2

List at least three design considerations for the Enterprise Edge WAN module.

Question 1 Answer

The identification of routing protocols and IP addressing is the final step in the Cisco eight-step approach for Enterprise Edge design. The following are the eight steps:

1 Identify the characteristics of applications that are used in the Enterprise Edge functional area.

2 Design the WAN's topology.

3 Identify required service provider features.

4 Identify Layer 2 technology.

5 Identify Layer 1 technology.

6 Identify required WAN, remote access, and Internet features.

7 Select appropriate Cisco hardware and software.

8 Identify routing protocols and IP addressing.

Question 2 Answer

The following are critical factors to consider when designing a site-to-site WAN:

- **Bandwidth (BW)**—Enough BW to support application demands

- **Link quality**—High-quality link to ensure packet delivery

- **Reliability**—A highly reliable and available link to ensure the delivery of packets

- **Layer 2 protocol characteristics**—The unique features offered by various data link layer protocols

- **Always-on or on-demand characteristics**—The characteristic of a link that determines whether it is always up, or only when needed

- **Cost**—Fixed (for example, one-time purchase) and recurring (for example, monthly service provider fees) expenses

Question 3

In the Enterprise Edge, when should redundant links be used to connect a branch office WAN to the Regional Edge?

Question 4

Explain the need for redundant links between the Branch Edge and the Central Site Edge in an Enterprise Edge design.

Question 3 Answer

Redundancy is not usually required between the branch office WAN and the Regional Edge because the branch office does not act as an aggregation point for other routers. However, redundant links might be desirable if the branch office operation is mission-critical, or if several users are impacted.

Question 4 Answer

The Branch Edge is typically an aggregation point for other routers (for example, branch office routers). Therefore, many users are impacted if the Branch Edge cannot contact the central site. Redundant links between the Branch Edge and the central site edge increase the availability of the network for these users. Additionally, these redundant links can be leveraged by load-sharing traffic across the primary and backup links.

Question 5

Identify the topology that sites in the Enterprise WAN backbone typically use.

Question 6

List at least three criteria to consider when selecting a service provider for your Enterprise Edge design.

Question 5 Answer

The Enterprise WAN backbone serves as the core of a company's WAN. To maintain required levels of service between remote and branch locations, availability and throughput between these backbone sites is critical. Therefore, sites that comprise the Enterprise WAN Backbone are typically interconnected in a *full-mesh* topology to minimize delay, increase availability, and increase the network's overall throughput.

Question 6 Answer

If your network spans multiple geographical regions, WAN services that are available in one location might not be available in another. Consequently, you might have to negotiate with multiple service providers. Consider the following characteristics when selecting a service provider:

- **Price**—Both one-time and recurring costs.

- **Available speeds**—Enough speed to support application demands.

- **Offered features**—Features, such as traffic shaping, that vary based on the Layer 2-specific technology chosen.

- **Geographic availability**—Locations that a specific service provider offers a specific type of service.

- **Service Level Agreements (SLAs)** —A contract between the customer and the service provider that stipulates such terms as available bandwidth, network delay, availability of network services, and packet loss through the network.

Question 7

Identify which of the following data link layer technologies supports the lowest link quality: PPP, Frame Relay, ATM, or X.25.

Question 8

Some physical layer technologies are "always on," while others are "on-demand." From the following list, identify which physical layer protocols are always on and which are on-demand: leased line, DSL, dialup, ISDN, and optical.

Question 7 Answer

X.25 supports the lowest link quality because it was developed at a time when the quality of transmission facilities was much less than is commonplace today. As a result, X.25 incorporates more error checking than do the other listed protocols. However, this increased error checking increases overhead costs.

Question 8 Answer

A leased line is always on.

DSL is always on.

Dialup is on-demand.

ISDN's control channel (or the D Channel) is always on. However, ISDN's data channels (or the B Channels) are on-demand.

Optical is always on.

Question 9

What WAN technology offers "service classes" such as CBR, ABR, UBR, RT-VBR, and NRT-VBR?

Question 10

When should static routes be used in a site-to-site WAN design?

Question 9 Answer

Asynchronous Transfer Mode (ATM) uses one of five service classes to determine what priority level is given to various traffic types. ATM's service classes are described as follows:

- **CBR**—Guaranteed bandwidth for high priority traffic (for example, video)

- **RT-VBR**—Useful for latency-sensitive traffic (for example, voice)

- **NRT-VBR**—Assigns a medium priority to traffic that is not sensitive to latency

- **ABR**—Similar to VBR-NRT, ABR assigns a medium priority to traffic

- **UBR**—Gives "best-effort" priority to low priority traffic

Question 10 Answer

Static routing is appropriate for smaller environments that have few WAN connections. For example, consider a single link between a central site and a remote site. The central site could have a static route that points to the remote site's network, and the remote site's router could have a default static route that points back to the central site.

Question 11

List at least three questions that you, as a designer, should ask when selecting the IP addressing scheme for the WAN module in the Enterprise Edge.

Question 12

List the two primary categories of remote access networks.

Question 11 Answer

Consider the following questions when selecting an IP addressing scheme for the WAN module:

- How many devices does the network contain? (Note that it is a best practice to add 20 percent to this number to accommodate future growth.)

- How many sites does the network contain, and how many devices reside at each site?

- How many network addresses are available from the public numbering authority?

- What is the total number of addresses that are required for the network?

- Are public and/or private address spaces required?

- How will the IP addressing hierarchy be completed?

Question 12 Answer

Site-to-site and **user-to-site** are the two primary categories of remote access networks. Site-to-site remote access networks are useful for interconnecting geographically separated offices, while user-to-site remote access networks allow mobile users to connect back to the corporate network.

Question 13

List at least two technologies that can be used to provide remote dialup access to end users.

The Enterprise Edge

Question 14

Identify two technologies that can be used to provide remote broadband access to end users.

The Enterprise Edge

Question 13 Answer

Remote dialup access options include the following:

Modem—Slower speed with moderate cost

ISDN—Moderate speed with moderate cost

Cell phone—Low speed with high cost

Question 14 Answer

Remote broadband access options include

Digital subscriber line (DSL)/cable—Low to high speed with moderate cost

Satellite—Moderate to high speed with high cost

Question 15

What formula should you use to determine the total required bandwidth when provisioning bandwidth for the central site remote access connection?

Question 16

When designing the Internet connectivity module, what extra design requirement do you have for traffic flowing from the Internet into your site, versus traffic flowing from your site into the Internet?

Question 15 Answer

The bandwidth needed for the central site remote access connection depends on the number of users, the percentage of those users who ever use the network simultaneously, and the required per-user bandwidth. The formula to calculate the total required bandwidth is as follows:

Total BW = (Number of Users) * (Percentage of Users Logged In) * (Required BW per User)

Question 16 Answer

Security is a design requirement for traffic that flows from the Internet into your site, but not necessarily a requirement for traffic that flows from your site to the Internet. However, regardless of the traffic flow direction, you should be concerned with functionality, performance, scalability, availability, manageability, and cost effectiveness when designing the Internet connectivity module.

Question 17

Describe the difference between NAT overloading and dynamic NAT.

Question 18

What type of routing is used for a router pointing to an ISP in a single-homed configuration?

Question 17 Answer

NAT overloading uses a single outside public IP address to service requests for multiple inside IP addresses by building a table that keeps track of Layer 4 port numbers associated with each session. Note that NAT overloading is sometimes called Port Address Translation (PAT).

Dynamic NAT maps private inside IP addresses to a pool of public outside IP addresses.

Question 18 Answer

A *default route* pointing to the ISP is appropriate for an edge router in a single-homed configuration because, if there is only one path to the Internet, the router is not required to maintain a copy of the entire Internet routing table.

Question 19

What routing protocol is appropriate for a router that points to multiple ISPs in a multihomed configuration?

Question 20

Describe the purpose of the remote access and VPN module, which is part of the Enterprise Edge.

Question 19 Answer

The *Border Gateway Protocol (BGP)* is appropriate for a router that points to multiple ISPs in a multi homed configuration. BGP forwards traffic based on autonomous system (AS) paths. By configuring your AS for BGP, the Internet can see multiple paths through which your AS can be reached (for example, a path via each of your ISPs).

In this configuration, your site can still reach the Internet, and Internet users can still reach your site's resources in the event of a single failure between your AS and one of your ISPs. Additionally, a multi-homed design adds load balancing.

Question 20 Answer

The remote access and VPN module is the piece of the Enterprise Composite Network Model that allows end users to access resources remotely. Common components in this module include access servers (for authentication and authorization), firewalls, and Intrusion Detection Systems (IDSs).

Section 3
Network Management

Network management services help you proactively monitor, manage, configure, and even troubleshoot the enterprise network. CiscoWorks is the Cisco flagship network management product. However, CiscoWorks is not a single software package; it has multiple add-on modules, such as the LAN Management Solution (LMS) and the Routed WAN (RWAN) Management Solution.

CiscoWorks functions as part of an overall network management strategy that you devise for your network. This strategy identifies network management goals, policies, and procedures. For example, you must document a series of response steps to perform in the event of various "what if" scenarios.

The flash cards in this section review the components of a network management strategy. They also focus on the components of the CiscoWorks network management solution and design guidelines.

Question 1

The goals of network management can be summarized in the acronym FCAPS. Identify what each letter in FCAPS represents.

Network Management

Question 2

List at least four services that might be found in the Network Management module.

Network Management

Question 1 Answer

The ISO defined a framework for network management that is referred to as FCAPS. FCAPS is an acronym that represents the following:

- Fault Management
- Configuration Management
- Accounting Management
- Performance Management
- Security Management

Question 2 Answer

The following services are often found in a Network Management module:

- Authentication server
- Access control server
- Network monitoring server
- IDS director
- Syslog server
- System administration server

Question 3

What is the first CiscoWorks component installed on a management server, and what applications does it contain?

Question 4

Identify the three components that are packaged as part of the CiscoWorks LMS.

Question 3 Answer

The first CiscoWorks component installed on a management server is *CD One*, which includes the following applications:

- CiscoView
- CiscoWorks Management Server
- Integration Utility

Question 4 Answer

The CiscoWorks LAN Management Solutions (LMS) includes the following:

- Campus Manager
- nGenius Real-Time Monitor
- Device Fault Manager

Question 5

Describe the purpose of the CiscoWorks ACL Manager.

Question 6

How many managed network devices does a single instance of the CiscoWorks LMS support?

Question 5 Answer

The ACL Manager is part of the CiscoWorks RWAN product bundle, and it provides a convenient way to create, edit, and distribute access lists to multiple IOS devices.

Question 6 Answer

A single instance of the CiscoWorks LAN Management Solution (LMS) can support networks of up to *2000 managed devices* or 40,000 end-user stations.

Question 7

What is the Cisco recommendation for the maximum number of managed devices supported on a single RME server?

Question 8

What is the maximum number of devices that a single CiscoWorks Central Resource Management server should support?

Question 7 Answer

Cisco recommends a maximum of *500 managed devices* per RME server. However, on higher-end systems, that number could grow to as large as 1000 managed devices.

Question 8 Answer

A single Central Resource Management server can support up to *5000 user devices*. The Central Resource Management can, for example, act as a repository for inventory, configurations, changes, and software distribution.

Question 9

What is the approximate maximum number of devices supported in a single CiscoWorks management domain, running LMS or RWAN?

Network Management

Question 10

Describe how the CiscoWorks IPM determines network conditions for multiple traffic types.

Network Management

Question 9 Answer

A management domain divides management responsibilities (such as resource network management, campus network management, and device fault management) across multiple servers. However, the domain's maximum capacity is not greater than that of a single management server. Therefore, the approximate number of devices supported in a single management domain, running LMS or RWAN, is 2000.

Question 10 Answer

The Internet Performance Monitor (IPM) sends Service Assurance Agent (SAA) probes out into the network. These SAA probes can emulate the appearance of various traffic types, such as HTTP or VoIP. By discovering how the network treats these probes, you can more effectively monitor and troubleshoot network conditions for application-specific traffic.

Section 4

High Availability

Previously, you considered the Common Network Infrastructure portion of the Cisco AVVID model. Next, consider AVVID's Intelligent Network Services portion. These services build on top of the infrastructure, ultimately providing a foundation for AVVID's network solutions. High availability is one of those intelligent network services.

The converged nature of today's enterprise networks requires you to support voice, video, and data over the same network. Some applications are mission-critical, and as a designer, you must maximize network uptime.

The flash cards in this section identify high availability measurements, and they examine approaches to achieving high availability at Layers 1, 2, and 3. They also review design best practices.

Question 1

How much downtime per year is represented by a high availability measurement of "five nines?"

Question 2

Describe how the Mean Time To Repair (MTTR) measurement influences availability.

Question 1 Answer

The "five nines" refers to 99.999 percent uptime, which translates to 5 minutes of downtime per year. The "six nines" (or 99.9999 percent uptime) equates to only *30 seconds of yearly downtime*.

Question 2 Answer

Availability of a system increases as the Mean Time To Repair (MTTR) decreases. In other words, if a device can be repaired quickly, its uptime increases.

Question 3

Discuss how the Mean Time Between Failure (MTBF) measurement influences availability.

Question 4

Describe how a Standby Route Processor in a Layer 3 switch increases the switch's availability.

Question 3 Answer

Availability of a system increases as the Mean Time Between Failure (MTBF) increases because less frequent downtime translates to increased uptime.

Question 4 Answer

A Layer 3 switch can have an Active Route Processor (RP) and a Standby RP. If the Active RP fails, the Standby RP takes over switch operation. However, the Standby RP does not process packets when in standby mode.

Question 5

Identify the pros and cons of the active-active and active-standby models of NIC redundancy.

High Availability

Question 6

Identify a Cisco-proprietary and an industry standard approach to providing first hop redundancy (such as maintaining an IP address for a device's default gateway).

High Availability

Question 5 Answer

For redundancy, a server or end-user station can have an additional Network Interface Card (NIC). With the active-active implementation, both NICs are simultaneously active, thereby reducing downtime in the event of an NIC failure. However, because each NIC has its own Media Access Control (MAC) address and IP address, troubleshooting becomes more difficult.

The active-standby implementation places one of the NICs on standby. Therefore, the standby NIC does not forward packets until the active NIC fails. This cutover process introduces a slight delay for the active-standby implementation as compared to the active-active implementation. However, the active-standby approach maintains a common IP and MAC address, regardless of which NIC is active; this results in simplified troubleshooting.

Question 6 Answer

First hop redundancy means that a different fault gateway can service an end station that is pointing to a default gateway in the event of a failure. A Cisco-proprietary approach to first hop redundancy is the *Hot Standby Router Protocol (HSRP)*. An industry standard approach is the *Virtual Router Redundancy Protocol (VRRP)*.

Question 7

Describe the Cisco EtherChannel feature.

Question 8

Describe the advantage of Multiple Spanning Tree (IEEE 802.1s) over the Cisco Per-VLAN Spanning Tree.

Question 7 Answer

The EtherChannel feature allows a switch to logically combine multiple physical connections (up to eight) into a single logical channel. Not only does EtherChannel improve throughput between switches by load balancing across the physical links, but it also improves redundancy. Specifically, if a link within the EtherChannel fails, the remaining EtherChannel physical links carry all of the traffic.

Question 8 Answer

With the Cisco traditional Per-VLAN Spanning Tree approach, each VLAN required its own instance of Spanning Tree, even if some of those instances were identical. This increased the switch's CPU overhead. However, with Multiple Spanning Tree (MST), also known as IEEE 802.1s, you define the number of Spanning Tree instances you need and then assign VLANs to those instances. This approach reduces the CPU overhead that is required to maintain extra instances of Spanning Tree.

Question 9

What Cisco proprietary enhancement to the IEEE 802.1D STP is appropriate for Building Access switches and reduces STP convergence time to approximately 1 to 5 seconds in the event of an uplink failure?

Question 10

The availability of a switched infrastructure can be improved through the use of module redundancy and/or chassis redundancy. Contrast the characteristics of module redundancy with those of chassis redundancy.

Question 9 Answer

UplinkFast is a Cisco-proprietary feature that reduces the Spanning Tree Protocol (STP) convergence time between Building Access switches and Building Distribution switches to approximately 1 to 5 seconds. This reduced time is made possible because the Building Access switch cuts over to a blocked port when its root port goes down, and because the Building Access switch sends a series of multicast frames, with the source MAC addresses being the MAC addresses of the directly attached end-user stations. The flooding of these multicast frames quickly trains the other switches in the topology to reach the directly attached end-stations over the backup link.

Question 10 Answer

Module redundancy enhances high availability by having back-up modules within a chassis take over in the event of a module failure. For example, if a primary route processor fails, a standby route processor takes over. The operating system within the chassis determines the cutover time. This approach is typically cost effective because additional chassis do not have to be purchased.

Chassis redundancy enhances high availability by interconnecting redundant chassis via multiple links. For example, if a single chassis or a single link fails, there is still a path through the network. However, having additional chassis and links can increase complexity and expense.

Question 11

Identify the second step in the Cisco five-step high availability design process.

Question 12

Identify at least one design best practice for providing high availability in the server farm module.

Question 11 Answer

The second step in the Cisco five-step high availability design process is: **Identify the budget to fund high availability features**.

The following five design steps contain the Cisco high availability best practices:

1 Examine technical goals.

2 Identify the budget to fund high availability features.

3 Categorize business applications into profiles.

4 Establish performance standards for high availability solutions.

5 Define how to manage and measure the high availability solution.

Question 12 Answer

Design best practices for the server farm include the following:

- Have redundant components in networking devices.
- Provide redundant paths between devices.
- Optionally, use multiple NICs in the servers (i.e., dual homing).

Section 5

Network Security

Securing network resources is considered one of the Intelligent Network Services of AVVID. The importance of network security increased dramatically over the past two decades because of the increased availability of advanced hacking tools. Today, even an unsophisticated hacker can download tools from the Internet, perform reconnaissance on your network, and attempt to breach your network security.

The flash cards in this section identify security risks and possible mitigations against those threats. Cisco has also integrated the concept of network security into the Enterprise Composite Network Model by creating the SAFE blueprint, which identifies which devices reside in which Enterprise Composite Network Model module, the potential security threats for each module, and the mitigations that can be used within each module.

Question 1

Identify four common security threats to enterprise networks.

Network Security

Question 2

List at least three common components of a documented security policy.

Network Security

Question 1 Answer

Four common security threats to enterprise networks include the following:

Loss of privacy—For example, obtaining another user's password via eavesdropping

Data theft—For example, making a copy of a private document

Impersonation—For example, gaining access to restricted resources by pretending to be a different user

Loss of integrity—For example, manipulating data in transit

Question 2 Answer

A security policy should contain the following components:

- **Acceptable use policy**—How the network is to be used

- **Identification and authentication policy**—How a user's identity is verified

- **Internet use policy**—What actions are valid uses of the Internet

- **Campus access policy**—When a user is permitted to access campus resources from inside the campus

- **Remote access policy**—When a user is permitted to access campus resources from a remote location

Question 3

Name the four components in the Cisco
continuous security design process.

Network
Security

Question 4

List the Cisco five broad categories of security
solutions.

Network
Security

Question 3 Answer

Security design is a continual process; changes are made based on newly identified threats. The four steps in this continual process include the following:

- **Secure**—Apply security solutions.

- **Monitor**—Observe the operation of the security solutions.

- **Test**—Verify the network's integrity by testing various methods of compromising the network.

- **Improve**—Repeat this process again based on the results of the testing.

Question 4 Answer

Cisco categorizes security solutions into the following five categories:

1. **Secure connectivity**—Protecting information from eavesdropping

2. **Perimeter security**—Ensuring that only authorized users access network resources

3. **Intrusion protection**—Uses technologies such as vulnerability scanners to test the network's integrity

4. **Identity**—Uses access servers, such as the Cisco Secure Access Control Server (ACS), to authenticate and authorize users

5. **Security management**—Uses tools to analyze and manage security solutions on an enterprise-wide basis, perhaps via a GUI

Question 5

List at least two ways to mitigate the security threat that is introduced by the presence of a packet sniffer on the network.

Question 6

What is the only security mitigation for a man-in-the-middle attack?

Question 5 Answer

Packet sniffers can capture packets that flow across the network. The following are approaches to mitigate this threat:

- Use authentication
- Use switches instead of hubs
- Use anti-sniffer tools
- Use cryptography

Question 6 Answer

Cryptography is the only mitigation for a man-in-the-middle attack (for example, packets are intercepted as they flow through the network).

Question 7

Identify two types of Cisco firewalls from which you can select.

Question 8

What are two types of Intrusion Detection Systems?

Question 7 Answer

Cisco offers the *PIX Firewall* as a standalone firewall appliance. However, for a personal firewall or a small network's firewall, you might select the *IOS Firewall*, which is a Cisco router running a version of the IOS that contains the Firewall feature set.

Question 8 Answer

Cisco offers both *host-based* and *network-based* Intrusion Detection Systems (IDSs). Host-based IDS is software that you install on a host to protect that host from attack. Network-based IDSs use hardware devices to compare packets against signatures of "well-known" attacks. After an attack has been identified, the IDS can send an alarm, send a TCP Reset, or block traffic from the offending device. The network-based IDS hardware can be a standalone appliance or a module in a Catalyst switch.

Question 9

In terms of security, what does AAA stand for?

Question 10

Which of the following AAA protocols is the most secure?

- RADIUS
- TACACS+

Question 9 Answer

AAA stands for *Authentication*, *Authorization*, and *Accounting*. Authentication validates that a user is who he says he is. Authorization specifies what a particular user can do. Accounting keeps track of what a user does.

Question 10 Answer

TACACS+ is more secure than RADIUS because it encrypts all the traffic sent between the Cisco device and the TACACS+ server. RADIUS only encrypts the access-request packet from the client to the server.

Question 11

List at least two goals of IPSec.

Question 12

**How many secure tunnels does IPSec establish
between two peers?**

Question 11 Answer

The four primary goals of IPSec are as follows:

- **Data confidentiality**—Scrambles data so eavesdroppers cannot interpret it

- **Data integrity**—Uses hashing algorithms to ensure the data was not manipulated

- **Data origin authentication**—Verifies that the packet came from the person from whom you think it came

- **Anti-replay**—Prevents packets that have been captured by a network sniffer from being replayed to spoof the entry of valid credentials

Question 12 Answer

IPSec establishes two secure tunnels between two peers—specifically, it creates an Internet Key Change (IKE) phase I tunnel and an IKE phase II tunnel.

Question 13

Explain the purpose of the Authentication Header (AH) and Encapsulating Security Payload (ESP) protocols.

Network
Security

Question 14

Define SAFE in the context of security.

Network
Security

Question 13 Answer

Both the AH protocol and the ESP protocol can be used as part of IP Security (IPSec) to *verify a packet's integrity*.

Question 14 Answer

SAFE is the Cisco blueprint for designing secure networks. The SAFE architecture categorizes devices and security threats into modules of the Enterprise Composite Network Model. For a comprehensive examination of the SAFE blueprint, examine the following link: http://www.cisco.com/go/safe.

Section 6

Quality of Service

Not all applications coursing through your network need the same priority level. VoIP traffic typically needs much higher priority than, FTP traffic for example. Also, different applications might require different amounts of bandwidth. Fortunately, QoS mechanisms allow you to customize the priority and bandwidth given to your various traffic types.

The flash cards in this section review the need for QoS and numerous categories of QoS tools, such as classification and marking, congestion avoidance, congestion management, traffic conditioning, signaling, and link-efficiency mechanisms. Finally, you are challenged to recall QoS design best practices.

Question 1

List three problems that might impact latency-sensitive applications in a network without QoS enabled.

Quality of Service

Question 2

Name the two broad categories of QoS tools.

Quality of Service

Question 1 Answer

In the absence of QoS, applications can suffer from one or more of the following:

- **Delay (latency)**—Excessive time required for a packet to traverse the network

- **Delay variation (jitter)**—The uneven arrival of packets, which the listener can interpret as dropped voice packets in the case of VoIP

- **Packet loss**—Dropping packets, especially problematic for UDP traffic (such as VoIP), which does not retransmit dropped packets

Question 2 Answer

The two broad categories of QoS tools are

- Integrated Services (IntServ)
- Differentiated Services (DiffServ)

However, more specific categories include the following:

- Classification and marking
- Congestion avoidance
- Congestion management
- Traffic conditioning
- Signaling
- Link-efficiency mechanisms

Question 3

How many priority levels can be specified using the DSCP form of packet marking?

Question 4

Where should a trust boundary be placed in your QoS design?

Question 3 Answer

The DSCP uses the six left-most bits in an IPv4 header's type of service (ToS) byte. These six bits have 64 possible binary combinations. Therefore, DSCP can specify up to **64 levels** of priority (0-63).

Question 4 Answer

A trust boundary is placed *as close to the source as possible*, at a device you trust to make marking decisions. For example, you might not trust a user's PC, but you might trust a Cisco IP phone on that user's desktop to make appropriate marking decisions. In that instance, you place the trust boundary at the Cisco IP phone.

Question 5

In terms of QoS, what primary congestion avoidance does Cisco use?

Question 6

What is the preferred congestion management tool for VoIP traffic?

Question 5 Answer

Weighted Random Early Detection (WRED) is the primary Congestion Avoidance tool used by Cisco. WRED prevents an interface's queue from filling to capacity by discarding packets more aggressively as the queue depth increases, based on priority markings.

Question 6 Answer

Low latency queuing (LLQ) is the Cisco preferred queuing (or congestion management) approach for VoIP traffic. With LLQ, you can define up to 64 classes of traffic (including a default class) and specify bandwidth guarantees for each class. With LLQ, you can also configure one or more of the traffic classes as a priority class.

Question 7

The traffic-conditioning category of QoS tools limits bandwidth for specified traffic types. List two categories of traffic conditioning tools.

Quality of Service

Question 8

Is RSVP considered an IntServ tool or a DiffServ tool?

Quality of Service

Question 7 Answer

Policing and shaping are both traffic conditioning tools that limit bandwidth usage. Examples of policing tools include class-based policing and committed access rate (CAR). Shaping tools include, for example, Frame Relay Traffic Shaping (FRTS), class-based traffic shaping, and generic traffic shaping.

Question 8 Answer

The RSVP, which uses signaling, is considered an *Integrated Services (IntServ)* tool.

Question 9

Describe the purpose of link fragmentation and interleaving (LFI).

Question 10

RTP Header Compression (cRTP) can compress a VoIP header from approximately 40 bytes down to what size?

Question 9 Answer

LFI fragments large payloads on low-speed links (for example, less than 768 kbps) and interleaves smaller packets among the fragments. This decreases the serialization delay that latency-sensitive traffic might experience.

Question 10 Answer

cRTP compresses the combined IP, UDP, and RTP header (approximately 40 bytes in size) down to approximately *2 to 4 bytes*.

Question 11

List at least two questions to ask as you design a QoS solution.

Question 12

Identify at least two QoS functions recommended for building access module switches.

Question 11 Answer

When designing a QoS solution, ask the following questions:

- What problems do the QoS tools need to solve?
- Will the IntServ or DiffServ model be used?
- How should the problem be solved?
- How do different solutions compare in terms of performance and cost?

Question 12 Answer

QoS functions recommended for a building access module switch include a switch's ability to do the following:

- Support multiple VLANs
- Manipulate markings provided by end-user systems
- Create a trust boundary close to the source

Question 13

Identify at least two QoS functions recommended for a building distribution module switch.

Question 14

Identify two QoS tools that are appropriate for use in campus backbone switches.

Question 13 Answer

QoS functions recommended for a building distribution layer switch include a switch's ability to do the following:

- Be QoS-enabled.

- Remark Layer 2 QoS markings (that is, class of service) to Layer 3 QoS markings (such as DSCP).

- Configure ports to trust appropriate QoS markings (such as CoS or DSCP).

Question 14 Answer

A campus backbone switch can be enabled for high-speed queuing (such as *LLQ*) and intelligent discard (such as *WRED*). However, the campus backbone is concerned with high-speed transport, not packet manipulation. Therefore, you do not want to mark traffic on the campus backbone.

Section 7

IP Multicasting

IP multicast technologies allow a source to send traffic to a large number of receivers efficiently. Examples of IP multicast applications include a company's CEO sending a corporate-wide video to thousands of receivers, or a Cisco CallManager sending music on hold to multiple IP phones.

The flash cards in this section review the need for and challenges of IP multicast technologies. It examines the protocols required to support IP multicast, and challenges you with IP multicast design guidelines.

Question 1

Describe the potential benefit of multicast versus unicast or broadcast.

Question 2

What range of IP addresses is reserved for IP multicast addresses?

Question 1 Answer

A video feed being sent to multiple users in your organization could consume a tremendous amount of bandwidth if the video to each receiver were unicast. A broadcast sends the packets to devices that do not want the packets. Fortunately, multicast can send a single copy of each packet from the source to only those devices that want to receive the packet.

Question 2 Answer

IP multicast uses Class D IP address, which are in the range of 224.0.0.0 through 239.255.255.255.

Question 3

Name at least two drawbacks of IP multicast technologies.

Question 4

Describe the purpose and operation of a multicast RPF check.

Question 3 Answer

IP multicast uses UDP, which is "unreliable." Therefore, WRED, which works with the TCP slow start mechanism, cannot be used as a congestion avoidance mechanism for IP multicast. With redundant pathing in the network, there is the potential that multiple copies of an IP multicast packet will be received, and the potential for IP multicast packets to arrive out of order.

Question 4 Answer

A Reverse Path Forwarding (RPF) check combats the issue of receiving duplicate packets in an IP multicast network. Cisco routers use the RPF check mechanism to determine whether a multicast packet is entering a router on the appropriate interface. An RPF check examines the source address of an incoming packet and checks it against the router's unicast routing table to see what interface should be used to return to the source network. If the incoming multicast packet is using that interface, the RPF check passes, and the packet is forwarded. If the multicast packet is coming in on a different interface, the RPF check fails, and the packet is discarded.

Question 5

Discuss the characteristics of a multicast source distribution tree.

IP Multicasting

Question 6

Describe the concept of a multicast shared distribution tree.

IP Multicasting

Question 5 Answer

A source distribution tree creates a loop-free path from each IP multicast source router to the last-hop router (or the router attached to the receiver). If multiple sources contain the same content, multiple trees are created, one from each source router to the last-hop router. As a result, routers have increased memory utilization. However, the source distribution tree does create an optimal path between each source router and the last-hop router.

Question 6 Answer

A shared distribution tree uses the concept of a rendezvous point (RP). Source routers (or the routers that are attached to the source) create a source distribution tree to the RP, which then forwards the multicast traffic down a shared tree to all of the last-hop routers (or the routers that are attached to receivers). Because the last-hop routers do not have a multicast routing entry for each server, and because they are using a wildcard entry to represent all sources for a multicast group, there is less memory overhead on the routers. However, because IP multicast packets all flow through the RP, a shared distribution tree might suffer from a sub-optimal path.

Question 7

Identify where you would use PIM-DM and PIM-SM in a multicast network design.

Question 8

Routers and Layer 2 switches can run what Cisco proprietary protocol to inform the Layer 2 switch that some of its interfaces are connected to multicast receivers?

Question 7 Answer

PIM Dense Mode (DM) uses the source distribution tree approach, which uses a flood and prune behavior. Because of the increased bandwidth utilization and memory overhead, PIM-DM is only recommended for use on small pilot networks.

PIM Sparse Mode (SM) uses the shared distribution tree approach, thereby avoiding PIM-DM's flood and prune behavior and using bandwidth more efficiently. However, PIM-SM takes it a step further by performing SPT (Shortest Path Tree) switchover. Specifically, after a last-hop router (or a router attached to a receiver) learns the identity of a source router (or a router attached to a source), it forms a SPT directly to the source router. As a result, PIM-SM still gives you the benefit of optimal pathing, while avoiding the flood and prune behavior.

Question 8 Answer

Typically found on lower-end switches, the **Cisco Group Management Protocol (CGMP)** is a Cisco proprietary protocol that allows the router to send two MAC addresses to the switch when the router receives an IGMP Report from a joining device. One of those MAC addresses is the Unicast Source Address (USA), which is the MAC address of the device that wants to join the group. The switch already knows, from its CAM table, to which interface that MAC addresses attached. The other MAC address is the GDA, which is the multicast group's MAC address. Therefore, when a switch receives a frame that is destined for a particular multicast MAC address, the switch knows the interface or interfaces to which the frame should be forwarded.

Question 9

In terms of multicast networks, describe the purpose and operation of IGMP snooping.

Question 10

List and describe at least two interdomain multicast routing protocols.

Question 9 Answer

IGMP snooping is a method of training a switch about which of its interfaces are connected to multicast receivers. However, IGMP snooping acts independently of router operations and is therefore even compatible with non-Cisco routers.

The switch enabled for IGMP snooping eavesdrops in on the IGMP messages that are being exchanged between receivers and a router. By watching those IGMP packets, the switch can determine which of its interfaces are connected to receivers for particular multicast groups.

Question 10 Answer

You need an interdomain multicast routing protocol for efficient multicast operations between BGP (Border Gateway Protocol) autonomous systems. Following are three interdomain multicast routing protocols, one of which is still in development, and two that can be used today:

- **Border Gateway Multicast Protocol (BGMP)**—With the goal of becoming a multicast routing protocol that can scale to the global Internet, BGMP is still in development.

- **Multicast BGP (MBGP)**—MBGP is an extension of BGP that allows autonomous systems to exchange multicast RPF information as MBGP multicast NLRI (Network Layer Reachability Information).

- **Multicast Source Discovery Protocol (MSDP)**—MSDP works with PIM-SM to allow rendezvous points (RPs) in one domain to announce their sources to another domain.

Question 11

In a multicast network design, what version of IGMP is required to support SSM?

Question 12

In a multicast network, IGMP is used between multicast receivers and multicast routers. With IGMP Version 1 configured with default settings, what is the maximum amount of time that can elapse before a router realizes that a receiver has left the multicast group?

Question 11 Answer

Source-Specific Multicast (SSM) requires *IGMP Version 3*. SSM allows a receiver to specify that it wants to receive content for a multicast group from a specific source. As a result, servers with different content can simultaneously transmit to the same multicast group address.

Question 12 Answer

Nearly *three minutes* can elapse before an IGMP Version 1 router realizes that a receiver left. By default, the router sends IGMP queries every 60 seconds. If two queries are sent and not responded to, the router concludes that a receiver left the group.

Consider a receiver that receives an IGMP query from the router to see whether the receiver still wants to belong to a group. If the receiver responds that it still wishes to belong, but shuts down its multicast application a split-second later, the router does not even recheck that device until nearly a minute later. After nearly 60 seconds elapse, the router again sends an IGMP query, and the receiver does not respond, which constitutes the first missed query. After another 60 seconds elapse, the router sends another IGMP query, to which the receiver does not respond. Finally, 60 seconds after the second IGMP query was sent, the router sees that there have been two missed queries and prunes the interface.

Question 13

Three different versions of the IGMP can be used in multicast networks. List an enhancement of IGMP Version 2 over IGMP Version 1.

IP Multicasting

Question 14

List at least three steps for designing an IP Multicast network solution.

IP Multicasting

Question 13 Answer

IGMP Version 2 *sends group-specific queries* and *supports the sending of "leave" messages* to inform the router of a receiver's departure from the multicast group.

Question 14 Answer

The following are six steps for designing an IP Multicast network solution:

1 Identify the multicast traffic's source.

2 Identify which receivers can receive traffic for the group.

3 Specify how receivers join the group.

4 Select PIM Dense Mode (PIM-DM) or PIM Sparse Mode (PIM-SM) as the router-to-router multicast protocol.

5 If PIM-SM is used, identify one or more rendezvous points (RPs).

6 Provision bandwidth on links to support multicast traffic.

Question 15

Where should RPs be placed in a small campus multicast network design?

Question 16

Where should RPs be placed in a large campus multicast network design?

Question 15 Answer

In a small campus design, any single RP could simultaneously support all IP multicast sessions. The RP or RPs should be placed in the building distribution module. However, in some small campus designs, you might have a collapsed core, in which the building distribution module and the campus backbone module are one in the same. In such a scenario, RP can be placed in the campus backbone.

Question 16 Answer

In a large campus design, distribute the load on your RPs by placing RPs throughout the network, giving different RPs responsibility for different ranges of IP multicast addresses.

Question 17

Where should RPs be placed in a design for a multicast network that spans a WAN?

Question 18

Identify a security concern with RPs in a multicast network design.

Question 17 Answer

In a WAN design, you do not want traffic from the source router (or the router that is attached to the source) to the RP flowing over the WAN. Such an approach is a very inefficient use of WAN bandwidth. Therefore, when designing an IP multicast solution for the WAN, place the RP as close to the source router as possible.

Question 18 Answer

Two security concerns with RPs include the following:

- An inappropriate source can send traffic to a multicast group.
- A rogue RP can be introduced into the network.

Access control lists (ACLs) are used to address both of these issues.

Section 8

VPNs

Traditionally, geographically separated corporate sites interconnected via a private WAN. Remote users (or telecommuters) used technologies such as dialup to access a modem bank that was located at the corporate headquarters. However, with the advent of VPNs, sites can securely connect with other sites, and users can securely connect with the corporate network over the public Internet. VPNs are far more scalable and less expensive than the legacy approaches mentioned previously.

The flash cards in this section identify the components of a VPN and review VPN design considerations. The design process for a VPN depends on the type of VPN being constructed—either a site-to-site or remote access VPN. These flash cards challenge you to identify specific issues for each VPN type.

Question 1

List and describe the two primary categories of VPNs that Cisco identifies.

VPNs

Question 2

A GRE tunnel supports what types of traffic that are not supported by an IPSec tunnel?

VPNs

Question 1 Answer

The two primary categories of VPNs are

- **Site-to-site**—Interconnects two sites as an alternative to a leased line at a reduced cost

- **Remote access**—Interconnects a remote user with a site as an alternative to dialup or ISDN connectivity at a reduced cost

Question 2 Answer

IP Security (IPSec) tunnels only support IP unicast traffic. Generic Router Encapsulation (GRE) tunnels add support for *multicast*, *broadcast*, and *non-IP traffic*.

Question 3

What is the purpose of 3DES in a VPN design?

VPNs

Question 4

As a design best practice, how many site-to-site tunnels require the use of a dedicated VPN concentrator versus an IOS router for termination?

VPNs

Question 3 Answer

Triple Data Encryption Standard (3DES) is an encryption standard that can be used to encrypt traffic that flows over a VPN. If packets are encrypted via 3DES, they are rendered virtually unusable to anyone who might intercept and capture the packets.

Question 4 Answer

An IOS router can be used to support up to 70 site-to-site tunnels. However, as a best practice, a dedicated VPN concentrator should be used for *70 or more site-to-site VPN tunnels*.

Question 5

What CiscoWorks module is designed for VPN and security management?

VPNs

Question 6

List at least two components of the CiscoWorks VPN/Security Management Solution.

VPNs

Question 5 Answer

In addition to other security services the *CiscoWorks VPN/Security Management Solution* module supports configuration, monitoring, and troubleshooting of VPNs.

Question 6 Answer

The CiscoWorks VPN/Security Management solution includes the following components:

- **VPN Monitor**—Monitors IPSec sessions on routers and concentrators

- **Cisco IDS Host Sensor**—Monitors security threats to critical servers

- **Cisco Secure Policy Manager (CSPM)**—Manages IDS, IOS, and PIX devices and can report intrusion alerts

- **Resource Manager Essentials (RME)**—Supports software distribution

- **CiscoView**—Graphically displays status information and allows you to configure a network element

Question 7

List at least two of the four key components that can comprise a site-to-site VPN.

Question 8

Name two advantages of using a site-to-site VPN versus a private WAN to interconnect multiple corporate sites.

Question 7 Answer

The four key components of a site-to-site VPN include the following:

1 Cisco head-end VPN routers

2 Cisco VPN access routers

3 IPSec and generic routing encapsulation (GRE) tunnels

4 Internet access

Question 8 Answer

A site-to-site VPN is *more scalable* and *less expensive* than a private WAN. However, a private WAN does have the advantage of being privately managed and is considered more secure.

Question 9

List at least two of the four primary steps for designing a site-to-site VPN.

Question 10

Describe a design scenario that is appropriate for a hub-and-spoke VPN topology.

Question 9 Answer

The four primary steps to site-to-site VPN design are

1 Characterize the application demands for the VPN.

2 Select a VPN topology between sites.

3 Add redundant connections.

4 Select a router for the head-end, based on anticipated VPN usage.

Question 10 Answer

A hub-and-spoke VPN topology is appropriate for a network with multiple remote sites that connect back to a central site, with little if any traffic traveling between remote sites.

Question 11

What is the main drawback of a full-mesh VPN design?

Question 12

Explain the recommendation of hard coding a VPN client's MTU to 1400 bytes.

Question 11 Answer

A full-mesh VPN design minimizes delay between remote sites and provides redundancy. However, a full-mesh VPN design is *not* scalable.

Question 12 Answer

Configuring a VPN client's Maximum Transmission Unit (MTU) size to 1400 bytes prevents the fragmentation that could occur after IPSec or GRE headers increase the packet size beyond 1500 bytes.

Question 13

List the two modes of IPSec over a VPN.

VPNs

Question 14

List three common tunneling protocols used by remote access VPN clients.

VPNs

Question 13 Answer

The two modes of IPSec over a VPN are

- **Tunnel Mode**—Encrypts each packet's header and payload
- **Transport Mode**—Only encrypts data

Question 14 Answer

VPN clients use the following three common tunneling protocols:

- IP Security (IPSec)
- Generic Router Encapsulation (GRE)
- Layer 2 Tunneling Protocol (L2TP)

Question 15

In a VPN design, why should a VPN concentrator be placed behind a router?

VPNs

Question 16

List at least three questions to ask when designing a remote access VPN.

VPNs

Question 15 Answer

A VPN concentrator should be placed behind a router to protect it from direct exposure to the public Internet.

Question 16 Answer

When designing a remote access VPN, answer the following questions:

- Is the primary goal remote access?
- What operating systems can be running on client devices?
- What VPN tunneling protocol is appropriate?
- What routing approach (such as static routes or a specific dynamic routing protocol) is appropriate for the VPN concentrator?
- How should user authentication be performed?
- Should the connection be a persistent connection (as in up all the time), or should it have a timeout?

Question 17

Identify at least two questions to ask when selecting a firewall for a remote access VPN design.

Question 18

What is the first step in capacity planning for a remote access VPN?

Question 17 Answer

Ask the following questions when selecting a firewall for a remote access VPN design:

- Does a firewall already exist in the topology?

- Is there an existing security policy specifying traffic that is permitted to pass through the firewall?

- Are firewall interfaces available to protect the VPN concentrator?

- Are two firewall interfaces available to protect both the public and private VPN interfaces?

- If only one firewall interface is available, which VPN interface should it protect?

Question 18 Answer

The first step in capacity planning for a remote access VPN is to *approximate the total number of users*.

Following is a complete list of capacity planning steps:

1 Determine the approximate number of total users.

2 Determine the approximate number of simultaneous users.

3 Identify the bandwidth of the existing ISP connection.

4 Determine the approximate bandwidth to be required for the ISP connection.

5 Specify how a user connects to the VPN.

6 Estimate future growth of the VPN.

Question 19

Explain how to enable an IPSec connection
through a router configured for PAT.

VPNs

Question 20

Define "split-tunneling" in the context of VPN
design.

VPNs

Question 19 Answer

IPSec runs directly on IP. Therefore, in a PAT configuration, NAT cannot examine port information, thus preventing the creation of IPSec connections. One way to fix this issue is called NAT Traversal, where IPSec peers negotiate an IPSec connection, determine whether NAT is in use, and use a UDP wrapper if NAT is in use. This UDP wrapper uses port 4500. This fix—sometimes called "packet stuffing"—allows only one IPSec connection through a NAT router running PAT.

Question 20 Answer

With split tunneling, only traffic that needs to flow over the VPN is sent over the VPN. Other traffic (such as web-browsing traffic) is sent unencrypted over the local default gateway, typically your ISP's next-hop router. Be aware that split tunneling introduces a potential security vulnerability. If a split-tunneling system were compromised from an attacker on the Internet, the attacker might have access (via the split-tunnel) to corporate resources that are available over the VPN.

Section 9

Wireless LANs

Wireless LANs (WLANs) lend themselves to the fluctuating demands for office space. WLANs can support network expansion into an unwired area of a building or interconnect two nearby buildings. However, because WLAN network traffic flows through the air, security is an important design consideration.

The flash cards in this section review the components and options of WLANs. You are challenged with design best practices. Also, because security is especially critical, you must distinguish between various WLAN security solutions and identify an appropriate use of each one.

Question 1

What is the purpose of an access point in WLAN design?

Question 2

Identify at least two factors that can affect the coverage area of a wireless access point.

Question 1 Answer

A wireless access point physically connects to the wired LAN network, and it has an antenna that allows communication with wireless clients. Therefore, an access point is the device that wireless clients pass through as they connect back to the wired LAN.

Question 2 Answer

The coverage area of a wireless access point varies depending on the following:

- Type and positioning of the WLAN antenna
- Power levels
- Structural barriers
- Required connection speed

Because of all the variables involved, a site survey is required to achieve an optimal coverage area.

Question 3

What is the maximum data rate of the 802.11b wireless standard?

Question 4

What is the maximum data rate of the 802.11a and 802.11g wireless standards?

Question 3 Answer

802.11b has a maximum data rate of 11 Mbps.

Question 4 Answer

802.11a and 802.11g both have a maximum data rate of 54 Mbps.

Question 5

Identify the 802.11 standard with which the 802.11g standard is backward compatible.

Question 6

Describe the purpose of a workgroup bridge in a WLAN design.

Question 5 Answer

Both 802.11b and 802.11g use a frequency band of 2.4 GHz, thereby enabling 802.11g to be backward compatible with 802.11b.

Question 6 Answer

A workgroup bridge typically contains a hub that provides connectivity to a few wired clients in a common location and provides access back to a wireless access point. With a workgroup bridge, a grouping of commonly located devices does not have to be converted to wireless clients. Rather, these devices can connect directly into the workgroup bridge.

Question 7

Describe the purpose of a wireless bridge in a wireless network design.

Question 8

What is the Cisco recommendation for the maximum number of devices associated with a wireless access point?

Question 7 Answer

A wireless bridge can be used to interconnect remote networks (up to a mile apart), in different buildings, that have a line of sight path between them.

Question 8 Answer

Because all devices on a wireless access point share bandwidth, Cisco recommends the maximum number of devices associated with a wireless access point to be in the range of *10 to 30 devices*.

Question 9

Identify the three non-overlapping 802.11b WLAN channels to use in an environment where the coverage area of three wireless access points overlap.

Question 10

Explain how Layer 2 and Layer 3 mobility can be achieved in a WLAN environment.

Question 9 Answer

WLAN channels 1, 6, and 11 are non-overlapping channels that can co-exist in the same area. Therefore, if the coverage areas of three wireless access points overlap, each of the three wireless access points should use one of the following channels: 1, 6, or 11.

Question 10 Answer

Layer 2 mobility is built into the Cisco wireless access points and allows you to move between wireless access points in the same VLAN while maintaining connectivity. Layer 3 mobility is possible through the use of an IOS feature known as Mobile IP. Mobile IP allows devices to retain their IP address, regardless of where in the network they are physically located.

Question 11

Describe the challenge of sending multicast traffic over a wireless LAN.

Question 12

What is the maximum number of IP phones that should be associated with a single WAP?

Question 11 Answer

All wireless clients associated with a WAP share the same bandwidth. Therefore, even if only one user on a WAP participated in a multicast session, all users connected to that WAP are impacted.

Question 12 Answer

Because VoIP traffic is latency-sensitive, and because bandwidth is shared among all devices that are associated with a single wireless access point (WAP), Cisco recommends that you associate no more than *seven* IP phones with a single WAP.

Question 13

How does the EAP improve wireless LAN security?

Question 14

How can IPSec be used to enhance wireless LAN security?

Question 13 Answer

EAP allows a wireless client and a wireless access point to mutually authenticate each other using a protocol such as 802.1x or RADIUS.

Question 14 Answer

Just as it can be created in a wired network, an IPSec VPN tunnel can be created in a WLAN environment to secure WLAN transmissions.

Question 15

Why are Static WEP keys considered a poor security solution for enterprise WLANs?

Question 16

What design would you recommend for an 802.11b WLAN that must support a large conference room with up to 50 simultaneous users?

Question 15 Answer

Static WEP uses a key that is manually configured on every wireless client and wireless access point. Static WEP keys are not considered to be a viable solution for enterprise WLANs because, if a laptop configured with the static WEP key is lost or stolen, all the wireless clients and wireless access points must be manually reconfigured with another static WEP key. Also, a static WEP key can be intercepted and decrypted with tools that are freely available on the Internet.

Question 16 Answer

One possible design for a conference room that must support 50 simultaneous users is to place two or three wireless access points (WAPs) in different corners of the conference room. Each of the WAPs must operate on a unique, non-overlapping channel—channel 1, 6, or 11.

Question 17

What wireless device would you recommend for interconnecting the networks in two buildings if there is a line of sight path between the buildings and the buildings are half a mile apart?

Question 18

What WLAN security feature would you recommend for a telecommuter with a single wireless laptop device?

Question 17 Answer

A *wireless bridge* is an appropriate solution for interconnecting buildings less than one mile apart that have a line of sight path between them. A wireless bridge extends the range of 802.11b by altering some of the timing constraints, thereby actually violating the 802.11 specifications.

Question 18 Answer

For a single wireless client in a telecommuter environment, you could use a *128-bit Static WEP key* for authentication between a wireless laptop and a wireless access point because you are not trying to protect corporate resources at the telecommuter's home. However, as the telecommuter connects back to the corporate network, the wireless laptop should communicate via an encrypted VPN connection.

Section 10

IP Telephony

The Cisco IP telephony technologies can replace traditional corporate telephony systems, typically including PBX. The core of the Cisco IP telephony solution is the Cisco CallManager (CCM); it is responsible for call routing, similar to the legacy PBX. Also, Cisco IP phones can replace analog phones.

The flash cards in this section review the components of an IP telephony network, including hardware and software options. Gateway control protocols are contrasted. In addition to other design best practices, various CCM deployment models are examined. The scalability limitations of the Cisco CallManager vary based on the CCM version and the underlying server platform (such as the Media Convergence Server). However, these flash cards reflect the specifications of Cisco CallManager version 3.1.

Question 1

Describe the Cisco CallManager's role in an IP telephony network.

IP Telephony

Question 2

What VoIP component converts voice calls between the PSTN and the IP telephony network?

IP Telephony

Question 1 Answer

The Cisco CallManager (CCM) replaces the legacy PBX's call processing role. Also, IP phones register with a CCM.

Question 2 Answer

A *gateway* converts between media types. For example, a gateway might have analog or digital Public Switched Telephone Network (PSTN) interfaces, in addition to an Ethernet interface that connects to an IP telephony network.

Question 3

In an IP telephony network, what hardware component is used for transcoding, media termination points, and hardware conference bridges?

Question 4

What is the maximum number of IP phones that can register with a single Cisco CallManager server running version 3.1 of the CallManager software?

Question 3 Answer

Digital Signal Processors (DSPs) add processing horsepower to an IP telephony solution. For example, DSPs can perform transcoding operations and act as media termination points (MTPs) or a hardware conference bridge.

Question 4 Answer

As of Cisco CallManager (CCM) version 3.1, a maximum of 2500 IP phones could register with a single CCM server.

Question 5

What is the maximum number of IP phones that can register with a cluster of Cisco CallManagers running version 3.1 of the CallManager software?

Question 6

List the four Cisco CallManager deployment models.

Question 5 Answer

As of Cisco CallManager (CCM) version 3.1, a maximum of *10,000* IP phones could register with a CCM cluster.

Question 6 Answer

A Cisco CallManager (CCM) network can be designed based on one of the following four models:

1 **Single-Site**—IP phones and CCMs located at a single site.

2 **Centralized call processing**—IP phones at multiple sites and all CCMs at a single site.

3 **Distributed call processing**—IP phones and CCMs at multiple sites.

4 **Clustering over the WAN**—IP phones and CCMs at multiple sites, with all CCMs logically assigned to the same cluster.

Question 7

Identify at least two VoIP gateway selection considerations.

Question 8

List at least three gateway-signaling protocols that are commonly used in Cisco IP telephony networks.

Question 7 Answer

When selecting a VoIP gateway, consider the following:

- Voice, fax, and modem support
- Appropriate interface types (such as analog, digital, or Ethernet)
- Gateway signaling protocol support

Question 8 Answer

The following are four of the most common gateway signaling protocols used in Cisco IP telephony networks:

- **Simple Gateway Control Protocol (SGCP)**—Also known as "non-IOS MGCP," SGCP provides call control between a Cisco CallManager (CCM) and a gateway, such as a Catalyst 6500 Series switch.

- **Media Gateway Control Protocol (MGCP)**—MGCP acts as a signaling protocol between a CCM and an analog gateway.

- **H.323**—H.323 supports signaling between an IOS router gateway, configured with dial-peers, and a CCM.

- **Session Initiation Protocol (SIP)**—SIP is an IETF standard that uses an ASCII-based approach to exchanging call control messages.

Question 9

How much bandwidth does the G.711 CODEC use for the voice payload?

Question 10

Define the function of transcoding in an IP telephony design.

Question 9 Answer

64 kbps of bandwidth is required for the voice payload when using the G.711 CODEC. The G.711 does not compress voice. Therefore, G.711 is not typically used across the WAN. The G.729 protocol, which requires 8 kbps of bandwidth for the voice payload, is often appropriate for use over the WAN.

Question 10 Answer

Transcoding is the process of converting between low and high-compression CODECs. For example, if voice traffic was entering your network encoded with the G.729 CODEC, you could use transcoding to convert the encoding to the G.711 CODEC, if required. Digital Signal Processors (DSPs) perform transcoding.

Question 11

What CODEC must all conference call participants use if the Cisco CallManager is acting as a software conference bridge?

Question 12

Identify the Cisco product that provides converged messaging services (such as for fax messages and voice mail).

Question 11 Answer

All conference call participants must use the G.711 CODEC if the Cisco CallManager (CCM) is acting as a software conference bridge. This limitation results from the CCM's inability to transcode between low and high-compression CODECs.

Question 12 Answer

The *Cisco Unity* product is a converged messaging system that provides a single repository for multiple messaging types. For example, a user can retrieve e-mail over the phone via text-to-speech conversion.

Question 13

How many Cisco CallManager servers are recommended to support up to 2500 IP phones?

Question 14

How many Cisco CallManager servers are recommended to support up to 10,000 IP phones?

Question 13 Answer

Two CCM servers are recommended to service up to 2500 IP phones. If one of the CCM servers fails, the other server can accommodate all 2500 IP phones. Note that these Cisco CallManagers belong to the same cluster.

Question 14 Answer

Eight CCM servers are recommended to service up to 10,000 IP phones. Four of the servers act as primary CCM servers, with IP phones registered with them. Two of the servers act as backup servers. One server acts as a dedicated publisher, and one server acts as a dedicated TFTP server. Note that these Cisco CallManagers belong to the same cluster.

Question 15

You are clustering Cisco CallManagers over a WAN, and there are 10,000 BHCAs. How much bandwidth is required for the WAN link to support the intra-cluster communication?

Question 16

When clustering Cisco CallManagers over the WAN, which failover approach is appropriate for up to six sites?

Question 15 Answer

900 kbps of WAN bandwidth is required for every 10,000 busy hour call attempts (BHCAs), when clustering Cisco CallManagers over a WAN connection. Also, the round-trip time (RTT) between any two CCMs in the cluster should be no more than 40 ms.

Question 16 Answer

When clustering over the WAN, the *Remote Failover* option is most appropriate for up to six sites, with a total of up to 10,000 IP phones for all sites combined. With 2500 to 5000 IP phones per site, the Local Failover option is more appropriate for two or three sites.

Question 17

What formula calculates the required bandwidth for voice traffic?

Question 18

What CiscoWorks component can place simulated IP phone calls (such as synthetic transactions)?

Question 17 Answer

The following formula can calculate required bandwidth for voice traffic:

Voice Bearer Traffic (bps) = (Packet Payload + Header Size in bits) * (Packet Rate per Second)

Question 18 Answer

The *CiscoWorks VoIP Health Monitor (VHM)* monitors the status, reachability, and environmental conditions of infrastructure hardware. VHM can also simulate an IP phone call to proactively test various configurations.

Question 19

Describe the purpose of SRST in an IP telephony design.

IP Telephony

Question 20

In an IP telephony design, what is an auxiliary VLAN?

IP Telephony

Question 19 Answer

SRST allows a remote site that does not have a Cisco CallManager to maintain a minimal level of call routing functionality in the event of a WAN failure. The SRST feature runs on a router that is configured as an H.323 gateway.

Question 20 Answer

An auxiliary VLAN is a VLAN that is used to transport voice packets. Specifically, an IEEE 802.1Q trunk is set up between a Cisco IP phone and a Catalyst switch. Over that trunk, data (from an upstream PC) is transported in one VLAN, and voice is transported in the auxiliary VLAN.

Section 11

Content Networking

As a designer, content networking technologies allows you to intelligently distribute content throughout the network, thereby reducing WAN bandwidth requirements. For example, a user could open a web browser and point to a particular site. A content networking component, called a "cache engine," might already have that site's content stored locally. Therefore, the cache engine satisfies the user's web request locally, without burdening the WAN.

The flash cards in this section challenge you to recall the components of the Cisco content networking solution and the functions of these components. The networking components all have an appropriate place and use within a network. You are therefore required to identify where to deploy various content networking components. Finally, you must identify appropriate content networking components to use for specific types of content (such as web, e-commerce, or streaming media).

Question 1

List the five components of the Cisco content networking solution.

Question 2

Content caching is a component of the Cisco content networking solution. Define the function of content caching.

Question 1 Answer

The Cisco content networking solution contains the following components:

1 Content caching

2 Content switching

3 Content routing

4 Content distribution and management

5 Intelligent network services

Question 2 Answer

Content caching stores content (such as graphics from a web page) in a cache engine. When a user requests content, rather than retrieving the content over the WAN, the content engine services the request locally if the content engine has the content. If the content engine does not have the content stored locally, it retrieves the content over the WAN and stores it locally so it can service future requests for that content.

Question 3

Describe the benefit of content switching in a content networking design.

Question 4

Identify an appropriate environment in which to deploy content routing.

Question 3 Answer

Content switching load balances requests across multiple content engines or servers that contain one content agent or server. As a result, content switching contributes to fault tolerance.

Question 4 Answer

Content routing is appropriate when users in multiple locations might be requesting the same content, and when the content exists in multiple locations. Content routing automatically locates the "best" content location for each client to use.

Question 5

What benefit does the Cisco Content Distribution Manager (CDM) offer?

Question 6

Where should you locate reverse proxy servers in a content networking design?

Question 5 Answer

The Cisco Content Distribution Manager (CDM) intelligently pushes content to geographically dispersed content engines. These content engines then serve up the content to local clients, thus reducing bandwidth demands on the WAN.

Question 6 Answer

Reverse proxy servers should be located in a *server farm*. The purpose of reverse proxy servers is to offload server content, thereby reducing demands on individual servers.

Question 7

In the Cisco content networking solution, how does transparent caching differ from proxy caching?

Question 8

Content routing directs user requests for content to an appropriate content engine. List the two modes of content routing.

Question 7 Answer

Transparent caching dynamically intercepts requests directed outside of the network and redirects those requests to a local content engine. However, proxy caching requires that a user's application (such as a browser) point directly to the content engine.

Question 8 Answer

The two modes of content routing are

1 **Direct Mode**—A user sends out a DNS request, which is forwarded to a local content router. The content router forwards the DNS request to multiple content routing agents at different locations, and the first content routing agent to respond is deemed the "best" site. The user's DNS request is then resolved to the IP address of the "best" site.

2 **WCCP Mode**—The Web Cache Communication Protocol (WCCP) allows a router to determine whether a request should be sent directly to the destination, or if it should be redirected to a content engine. If the content engine does not have the requested content, it retrieves the content and has it available for subsequent requests.

Question 9

What content networking component uses Self-Organizing Distributed Architecture (SODA)?

Question 10

According to a Cisco best practice for content network design, how much storage space (measured in hours) is recommended for a content engine to produce a significant bandwidth savings?

Question 9 Answer

The Cisco *Content Distribution Manager (CDM)* uses the SODA to keep track of what content is located on which content engine.

Question 10 Answer

Cisco recommends *24 to 72 hours* worth of storage space on a content engine to produce significant bandwidth savings.

Question 11

You are using content networking for web-caching purposes. Where should you place content engines?

Content
Networking

Question 12

You are designing a content network to support streaming media. Why might your design be a good candidate for a Cisco CDM?

Content
Networking

Question 11 Answer

Content engines should be strategically placed to prevent unnecessary WAN access. For example, remote offices are often appropriate locations for content engines because content engines allow much of the content to be served up locally.

Question 12 Answer

A CDM is often applicable for streaming media applications because it can intelligently push the content to remote content engines. Those content engines can then serve up the content to local users.

Section 12

Storage Networking

The need for storage in today's networks continues to grow. However, the approach of increasing storage by adding additional network servers does not scale well. Fortunately, the emergence of storage networking technologies allows you, as a designer, to incorporate dedicated storage devices into your design.

Two primary approaches to storage networking include Network Attached Storage (NAS) devices and storage area networks (SANs). Each approach has its own set of applications for which it is best suited. With the high-speed transfer rates required by most storage applications, bandwidth provisioning is a key design consideration.

The flash cards in this section confirm your understanding of the technologies surrounding storage networking and storage network design approaches, and when each approach is used. You must also recall questions to ask during the storage network design process.

Question 1

In the context of storage networking, what is a SAN?

Question 2

What is the purpose of a NAS device in a storage network?

Question 1 Answer

A SAN is an independent network designed specifically for interconnecting storage devices.

Question 2 Answer

A NAS device supports file storage over an IP network. For example, the NAS and a UNIX NFS volume might appear.

Question 3

What type of physical connection is typically used in a SAN to interconnect storage devices?

Question 4

You are considering using NAS devices in a storage network design. List at least two network applications that are appropriate for NAS devices.

Question 3 Answer

SANs typically use *Fibre Channel* to interconnect storage devices.

Question 4 Answer

Because NAS devices support file storage over an IP network, they are appropriate for applications such as file sharing, e-mail services, and web services.

Question 5

Identify the types of applications that benefit from a SAN, as opposed to benefiting from a NAS device, in a storage network design.

Question 6

How does Fibre Channel transfer data differently than a LAN transfers data?

Question 5 Answer

SANs are appropriate for high-volume, write-intensive applications, such as database applications.

Question 6 Answer

Fibre Channel transfers data in large blocks, without breaking it up into packets like a LAN does.

Question 7

Describe the purpose of Fiber Channel over IP (FCIP) in a storage network design.

Storage
Networking

Question 8

A storage network can use the Internet Small Computer System Interface (iSCSI) protocol to interconnect SCSI devices over an IP network. What is contained in an iSCSI packet?

Storage
Networking

Question 7 Answer

FCIP allows you to interconnect SAN islands over an IP network by encapsulating Fibre Channel communication in IP packets.

Question 8 Answer

iSCSI encapsulates *SCSI data and command frames* into IP packets.

Question 9

List at least two approaches for securing storage network transactions.

Question 10

Your storage network needs 400 Mbps of bandwidth between two switches; however, each switch only contains 100 Mbps interfaces. Without upgrading the switches' hardware, how can you meet the bandwidth demands of the storage network?

Question 9 Answer

To secure storage network transactions, consider isolating storage in a separate VLAN and using access control lists (ACLs) to limit access to storage resources. RADIUS or TACACS+ can be used to authenticate iSCSI connections, and IP Security (IPSec) can protect FCIP traffic as it tunnels across the network.

Question 10 Answer

In the situation presented, multiple 100-Mbps interfaces (four or eight, depending on the switch type) can be logically combined together in an EtherChannel. For example, four 100-Mbps interfaces could be combined to create a 400-Mbps EtherChannel interface. If the interfaces in the EtherChannel were configured for full duplex, then the maximum theoretical throughput would approach 800 Mbps.

Question 11

List at least two questions one should ask when designing a storage network solution.

Storage
Networking

Question 12

Identify an application that could benefit from a storage network that spans a WAN or a MAN.

Storage
Networking

Question 11 Answer

When designing a storage network solution, ask the following questions:

- Do applications require backup capabilities or realtime access?
- What are the traffic patterns for each application?
- How much bandwidth is required for each application?
- What special needs do the applications have for availability, security, and quality of service?

Question 12 Answer

Examples of WAN or MAN storage network applications include using a storage network for an *off-site backup* or for *consolidating storage* to support applications such as data mining. These applications are made possible with storage networking because technologies such as iSCSI or FCIP run over an IP network. Of course, sufficient bandwidth must be provisioned to accommodate application demands.

CCDP-ARCH Quick Reference Sheets

Network Architectures

AVVID

The Cisco Architecture for Voice Video and Integrated Data (AVVID) encompasses three primary areas:

- Network infrastructure
- Services
- Applications and solutions

The network infrastructure consists of the campus infrastructure, the Enterprise Edge, and the Service Provider Edge.

The services that enhance the network infrastructure include such components as network management, high availability, security, quality of service, and IP multicasting. Applications and services that leverage these services include IP telephony, content networking, and storage networking, for example.

Network Deployment Concerns

The design process is primarily concerned with the following items:

- **Performance**—Performance is measured in terms of responsiveness, throughput, and utilization.
- **Scalability**—Scalability is concerned with the ability to size the topology; addressing, and routing protocols to accommodate growth within the network.
- **Availability**—Availability focuses on device fault tolerance, redundant network links, rapid protocol convergence, and the ability to support network capacity demands.

Enterprise Composite Network Model

Traditionally, Cisco prescribed a three-layer model for network designers. Those three layers include the following:

- **Access layer**—Typically, wiring closet switches connecting to end-user stations.
- **Distribution layer**—An aggregation point for wiring closet switches, where routing and packet manipulation occur.
- **Core layer**—The network backbone, where high-speed traffic transport is the

However, this three-layer hierarchical approach has scalability limitations. Cisco developed the Enterprise Composite Network model for today's enterprise networks. The functional areas that comprise the Enterprise Composite Network include the following:

- **Enterprise Campus**—The portion of the network design that provides performance, scalability, and availability, and defines operation within the main campus.
- **Enterprise Edge**—An aggregation point for components at the edge of the network (such as Internet and WAN connectivity) that routes traffic to and from the Enterprise Campus function area.
- **Service Provider Edge**—The network that a service provider makes available (such as Frame Relay or ATM).

Enterprise Composite Network Model

Enterprise Campus	Enterprise Edge	Service Provider Edge
Management Module	E-Commerce Module	ISP Modules
Building Access Module	Internet Connectivity Module	Public Switched Telephone Network (PSTN) Module
Building Distribution Module	Remote Access/VPN Module	Frame Relay/ATM/PPP Module
Campus Backbone Module	WAN Module	
Server Farm Module		
Edge Distribution Module		

Enterprise Campus Components

When designing the Enterprise Campus Functional Area in the Enterprise Composite Network model, you must address four primary areas:

- **Campus Infrastructure Module**—Interconnects users and contains the following submodules:
  - **Building access**—Connects end-user devices into the network
  - **Building distribution**—Aggregates building access switches and performs Layer 3 switching (for example, routing) functions
  - **Campus backbone**—Provides high-speed, redundant connectivity between buildings

Server Farm Module

- **Edge Distribution Module**—Responsible for routing traffic between Enterprise Campus and the Enterprise Edge

Enterprise Edge Components

The Enterprise Edge, which is responsible for "funneling" traffic between the Enterprise Campus and the Service Provider Edge, has four modules that the enterprise network designer must address:

- **E-commerce**—Contains the servers that are used to provide an e-commerce presence for a company, including the following:
  - —Web servers
  - —Application servers
  - —Database servers
  - —Security servers

Campus Infrastructure Module

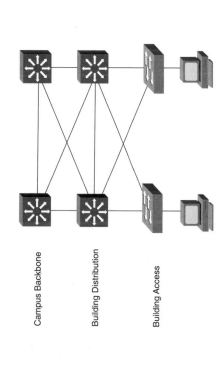

- **Network Management Module**—Responsible for campus-wide management functions, such as the following:
  - —Intrusion Detection Systems (IDS)
  - —Logging
  - —Authentication
- **Server farm module**—Contains campus servers that provide campus-wide services:
  - —Application servers
  - —File servers
  - —E-mail servers
  - —Domain Name System (DNS) servers

- **Internet connectivity**—Provides Internet-related services, including the following:
  - —E-mail servers
  - —DNS servers
  - —Public web servers
  - —Security servers
  - —Edge routers
- **Remote access and VPN**—Provides secure access for remote workers (such as telecommuters) or remote offices and includes components such as the following:
  - —Dial-in access concentrators
  - —VPN concentrators
  - —Firewalls and IDS systems
  - —Layer 2 switches
- **WAN**—Interconnects a main office with remote offices over various transport technologies, such as the following:
  - —Frame Relay
  - —ATM
  - —Point-to-Point Protocol (PPP)

Service Provider Edge Components

The Service Provider Edge is the one area of the Enterprise Composite Network module that is not explicitly designed. A service provider designs, owns, and operates the Service Provider Edge. However, the enterprise network designer can specify the type of connection to use for connecting to the service provider. Specifically, the Service Provider Edge modules include the following:

- Internet service provider (ISP)
- Public Switched Telephone Network (PSTN)
- Frame Relay/ATM/PPP

Steps to Campus Design

For a designer of enterprise networks, a logical step-by-step methodology is critical to minimizing the time required to revisit and update earlier stages of the design. Cisco provides the following seven-step design process:

1. Identify requirements of existing enterprise applications and data flows.
2. Design the logical network topology (for example, identify VLANs).
3. Design the physical network topology (for example, identify Layer 1–3 compo-

4. Identify Cisco devices that meet the previous criteria and diagram the network topology.
5. Select an appropriate IP addressing scheme.
6. Choose routing protocols.
7. Design the Edge Distribution module, which connects the Enterprise Campus to the Enterprise Edge.

Campus Design: Step 1

Identifying requirements of existing enterprise applications and data flows is the first step of the campus design methodology. Creating a spreadsheet to identify the specific properties of each enterprise application is often a useful approach.

The traffic an application generates is measured as an amount of data crossing a particular network link at a particular time. Therefore, application bandwidth demands vary based on such variables as the number of users, the type of application, and when the measurement was taken. Therefore, when analyzing traffic, take multiple measurements during various load conditions.

Campus Design: Step 2

The second step of the campus design methodology is to design the logical network topology. This process involves identifying which devices are placed in which VLANs. There are several VLAN segmentation approaches from which a designer can select:

- Define VLANs based on departments or organizational units.
- Define VLANs by application (for example, data, voice, or video).
- Create flat networks (only recommended for very small networks).

While creating a campus-wide VLAN with trunking technology is possible, it is not recommended. Because each VLAN is a "failure domain," the larger the VLAN, the larger the potential failure domain. Additionally, having a large VLAN diameter (that is, the maximum number of switches that must be traversed for any one point in the VLAN to reach any other point in the VLAN) negatively impacts the amount of time required for the Spanning Tree Protocol (STP) to converge. Three of the primary approaches to VLAN design include the following:

- One VLAN per switch (useful in access layer switches)
- Unique VLANs per switch
- VLANs spanning multiple access switches

Campus Design: Step 3

The third step of the campus design methodology is designing the physical network topology. This step involves selecting transmission media and data-link protocols, and identifying where in the network to deploy Layer 2 and/or Layer 3 switching.

Common Transmission Media choices include the following:

- **Twisted Pair**
  - —100 m distance limit
  - —1 Gbps speed limit
  - —Low cost
  - —Typically used for building access
- **Multimode Fiber**
  - —2 km distance limit (FastEthernet) or 550 m distance limit (Gigabit Ethernet)
  - —1 Gbps speed limit
  - —Moderate cost
  - —Typically used for building distribution and campus backbone

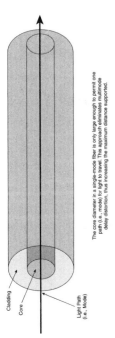

Multimode Fiber

Paths of Light (i.e., Modes)

Cladding

Core

The core diameter in a multimode fiber is large enough to permit multiple paths (i.e., modes) for light to travel. The might cause different photons (i.e., light particles) to take different amounts of time to travel through the fiber. As distance increases, this leads to multimode delay distortion. Therefore, multimode fiber has a distance limitation on approximately 2 km.

- **Single-Mode Fiber**
  - —40 km distance limit (FastEthernet) or 90 km distance limit (Gigabit Ethernet)
  - —Speed limit of 10 Gbps or greater
  - —High cost
  - —Typically used for building distribution and campus backbone

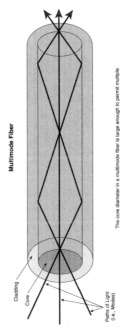

Single-Mode Fiber

Cladding

Core

Light Path (i.e. Mode)

The core diameter in a single-mode fiber is only large enough to permit one path (i.e., mode) for light to travel. This approach eliminates multimode delay distortion, thus increasing the maximum distance supported.

Common Data-link Protocol choices include the following:

- **Ethernet**
  - —10 Mbps
  - —Very low cost
  - —Typically used for building access
- **Fast Ethernet**
  - —100 Mbps
  - —Low cost
  - —Typically used for building distribution and campus backbone
- **Gigabit Ethernet**
  - —1000 Mbps
  - —Moderate cost
  - —Typically used for building distribution and campus backbone
- **10 Gigabit Ethernet**
  - —10,000 Mbps
  - —High cost
  - —Typically used for campus backbone

After selecting the transmission media and the data-link protocol, the enterprise network designer chooses a physical network segmentation strategy. Considerations include the following:

- **Broadcast domains**—Isolates broadcast through the use of Layer 3 switches.
- **Failure domains**—Limits the size of a potential failure domain to a single wiring closet switch, if possible.
- **Policy domains**—Defines allowed and denied traffic on an IP subnet (through the use of access control lists [ACLs])

Other physical design considerations include selecting a Spanning Tree Protocol (STP) approach. If supported on the switch hardware, the preferred STP approach is 802.1w (for example, Rapid Spanning Tree), which dramatically reduces STP convergence time. 802.1w also works well in conjunction with 802.1s (Multiple Spanning Tree), which allows VLANs to be assigned to configured STP instances.

When selecting between Layer 2 and Layer 3 switching, consider that Layer 3 switches works well in hierarchical networks and supports load balancing across multiple links. Therefore, Layer 3 switches are appropriate for the building distribution and campus backbone modules, while Layer 2 switching is appropriate for the building access and, in some cases, the campus backbone modules.

Campus Design: Step 4

The forth step of the campus design methodology is to identify Cisco devices that meet the design requirements. The Cisco Product Advisor is available on the Cisco website. The Product Advisor has a "Novice" mode that interviews the user about the use of the product being selected. An "Expert" mode is also available to the user who already knows such information as how many and what types of interfaces are required.

The Product Advisor can be found at http://www.cisco.com/en/US/products/products_cisco_product_advisor_tool_launch.html.

Campus Design: Step 5

The fifth step of the campus design is to select an appropriate IP addressing scheme. Consider the size of the network—specifically, the number of locations and the size of each location.

With the depletion of IPv4 address space, many designs might require you to use private address space. By using Network Address Translation (NAT) with Port Address Translation (PAT), a few public IP numbers can service multiple internal systems. However, some applications might not work well with PAT and thus require unique public IP

addresses. Therefore, you must understand the IP address requirements of the customer's network to select an appropriate mix of private and public address space.

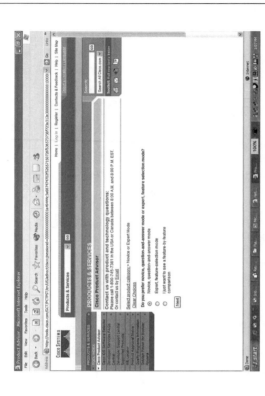

Campus Design: Step 6

The sixth step of the campus design is to choose the routing protocol(s) to be used. In a large, dynamic network, a dynamic routing protocol is more appropriate than static routing entries. However, static routing is still a viable alternative for smaller, non-growing networks or stub networks.

You might consider the following dynamic routing protocols:

- **RIP**—A distance vector routing protocol that is rarely used in a LAN environment because of its periodic advertisement of a router's entire routing table
- **IGRP**—A distance vector routing protocol with a more sophisticated metric than RIP; however, still suffers from slow convergence.

- **EIGRP**—A hybrid routing protocol that offers fast convergence and is very scalable.
- **OSPF**—A link-state routing protocol that offers fast convergence, is very scalable, and lends itself well to summarization through the use of "areas."
- **IS-IS**—A link-state routing protocol that is similar to OSPF and is appropriate for very large networks, but lacks full support for NBMA networks (such as Frame Relay).

Campus Design: Step 7

The seventh step of the campus design methodology is to design the Edge Distribution module. Typically, the Edge Distribution module consists of a Layer 3 switch. You can leverage the previous design decisions (for example, Layer 2 technology and supported routing protocols) along with the Cisco Product Advisor to select an appropriate Layer 3 switch for the Edge Distribution module.

Server Farm Design

The server farm is a mission-critical component in today's enterprise networks. Therefore, as an enterprise network designer, you should have very stringent design requirements for the server farm module. Typical objectives include the following:

- **Performance**—Providing sufficient capacity for traffic loads
- **Scalability**—Handling increases in traffic
- **Availability**—Assuring fault-tolerance in the design
- **Security**—Implementing physical and software security, in combination with a documented security policy
- **Manageability**—Monitoring server status, including the status of processes running on the server

Just as a building has a building access and a building distribution layer that connects back to the campus backbone, the server farm module also has a server farm access layer and a server farm distribution layer that connects back to the campus backbone. As with the building modules, the server farm typically uses Layer 2 switching at the access layer and Layer 3 switching at the distribution layer.

The Enterprise Edge

The Enterprise Edge functional area of the Enterprise Composite Network model includes e-commerce, VPN/remote access, and WAN modules. The Enterprise Edge functional area separates the Enterprise Campus from the Service Provider Edge.

Therefore, all traffic that flows between the Enterprise Campus and the outside world must flow through the Enterprise Edge.

Steps to Enterprise Edge Design

Just as Cisco provides a seven-step design approach for the Campus network, it also provides the following eight-step design approach for the Enterprise Edge:

1. Identify the characteristics of applications used in the Enterprise Edge functional area.
2. Design the WAN's topology.
3. Identify required service provider features.
4. Identify Layer 2 technology.
5. Identify Layer 1 technology.
6. Identify required WAN, remote access, and Internet features.
7. Select appropriate Cisco hardware and software.
8. Identify routing protocols and IP addressing.

Enterprise Edge Design: Step 1

You can use the same set of criteria to identify the characteristics of applications residing in the Enterprise Edge function area as you used for the Enterprise Campus functional area. Additionally, identify the typical size for various data types (for example, e-mail messages, spreadsheets, or database replications).

Enterprise Edge Design: Step 2

The second step in designing the Enterprise Edge is to design the WAN's topology. The following factors influence your decision:

- Bandwidth
- Link quality
- Reliability
- Data-link protocol characteristics
- Always-on or on-demand characteristics
- Cost

Typically, a large enterprise network's WAN topology is neither a pure full-mesh nor a pure hub and spoke design. Rather, in addition to a partial mesh approach, both approaches can be used.

Branch offices sit at the end of the network and do not typically act as aggregation points for other sites. Therefore, redundant links between the Branch Edge and the Regional Edge depends on the mission-critical nature of the traffic being transferred.

Regional offices aggregate traffic from specific branch offices. Because these locations carry traffic from multiple locations, redundant links from the Regional Edge to the Central Site Edge become more critical. To maximize the use of these redundant links, specify load sharing across the links.

Central site offices typically interconnect using a full-mesh design because of the volume of traffic flowing between each site. This interconnection of central site offices is called the *Enterprise WAN backbone*. The full-mesh design provides not only increased bandwidth to the network, but increased resilience in the event of a link or site failure.

Enterprise Edge Design: Step 3

Because availability of services varies by location, you might have to adjust the design decisions you made in Steps 1 and 2 based on your discussions with local service providers. When in negotiations with a service provider to provide service to your various sites, consider the following design criteria:

- Price
- Speed
- Features
- Available locations
- Service-level agreements (SLAs)—A contract with the service provider that specifies such parameters as bandwidth, delay, and packet loss

Enterprise Edge Design: Step 4

The forth step in designing the Enterprise Edge is to select the Layer 2 (that is, the data link layer) technology that is used to connect to the service provider. This decision relies heavily on the facts gathered in Step 3.

Common Layer 2 technologies include the following:

- **PPP**—Appropriate for router-to-router connections over dedicated leased lines or over ISDN
- **Frame Relay**—A switched protocol that forwards traffic between locations over Permanent Virtual Circuits (PVCs) based on DLCIs (Data Link Connection Identifiers)
- **ATM**—A cell-switching technology that uses 53-byte cells and was designed to take advantage of high-speed transmission media

- **X.25**—A legacy protocol that performs extra error checking, thereby making it appropriate for locations where the quality of the transmission media is in question

Of these Layer 2 technologies, ATM has the highest bandwidth, while X.25 has the lowest. However, because of its extra error checking, X.25 has the highest reliability. The costs of Frame Relay, ATM, and X.25 are considered moderate, and the cost of PPP is considered low.

Enterprise Edge Design: Step 5

Based on the Layer 2 technology identified in Step 4, the fifth step in designing the Enterprise Edge is to identify the Layer 1 (that is, the Physical Layer) technology. Common choices for Layer 1 technology include the following:

- **Leased lines**—Often used in conjunction with the PPP protocol for hub-and-spoke environments or as a backup link
- **Digital subscriber line (DSL)**—An "always-on" connection to the Internet that is available over telephone lines
- **Dialup**—A lower-speed solution that is useful for periodic connections to the corporate network (for example, a salesperson checking corporate e-mail from a hotel room)
- **ISDN**—An on-demand solution for connecting back to the corporate network; often used to transport video or to act as a backup link
- **Optical**—A high-bandwidth technology (such as SONET) that is useful for interconnecting central sites

Enterprise Edge Design: Step 6

The sixth Enterprise Edge design step is to identify required WAN, remote access, and Internet features. These features vary based on the Layer 2 technology you selected in Step 4. Following are some of the available features for the Layer 2 technologies, as we discussed previously:

- **PPP**
  - Multilink PPP (MLP)—Logically bundles multiple physical links together to aggregate bandwidth
- **Frame Relay**
  - Traffic shaping—Specifies the average amount of data send over the period of a second (that is, the CIR), and how much extra traffic is allowed to be sent in excess of the CIR (that is, the maximum burst size)

- **ATM**

  —Service classes—Five predefined quality of service designations that specify how much priority is given to cells in these classes

    — CBR—Guaranteed bandwidth for high priority traffic (for example, video)
    — RT-VBR—Useful for latency-sensitive traffic (for example, voice)
    — NRT-VBR—Assigns a medium priority to traffic that is not sensitive to latency
    — ABR—Similarly to VBR-NRT, assigns a medium priority to traffic
    — UBR—Gives "best-effort" priority to low priority traffic

- **X.25**

  —Rate—Provides lower traffic rates than are available for Frame Relay because of increased error-checking overhead

Enterprise Edge Design: Step 7

The seventh step in designing the Enterprise Edge is to identify appropriate Cisco solutions. As mentioned earlier, the Cisco Product Advisor identifies appropriate Cisco devices that meet the criteria you specify. The Product Advisor is a web-based tool that can operate in the Novice or Expert mode. The tool is available at the following URL:

http://www.cisco.com/en/US/products products_cisco_product_advisor_tool_launch.html.

Enterprise Edge Design: Step 8

The eighth and final step in designing the Enterprise Edge is identifying the appropriate routing protocol(s) and IP addressing schemes. Typical routing protocol approaches for use in the Enterprise Edge include the following:

- **Static routes**—Useful for flat and point-to-point networks
- **EIGRP**—Suitable for all network types
- **OSPF**—Suitable for all network types, with the exception of flat networks, because of OSPF's use of areas
- **RIPv2**—Suitable for all network types because of the addition of VLSM support in version 2

Keep in mind that RIPv2, like RIPv1, has a maximum hop count of fifteen. Therefore, RIPv2 is most appropriate for hub-and-spoke environments.

Ask the following questions when selecting an IP addressing scheme:

- How many devices are in the network? (Note that it is a best practice to add 20 percent to this number to accommodate future growth.)

- How many sites are in the network, and how many devices are located at each site?
- How many network addresses are available from the public numbering authority?
- What is the total number of addresses required for the network?
- Are public and/or private address spaces required?
- How will the hierarchical IP addressing be assigned?

Remote Access and VPN Module

When you are designing the remote access and VPN module in the Enterprise Edge, you must balance your users' with the IT concerns. For example, users want easy access to resources, while IT requires user authentication.

Your remote access design has four functional remote access areas to address:

1. **Remote access types**—Defines whether the connectivity is site-to-site or user-to-site
2. **Remote access connectivity options**—Defines the network that is used to remotely connect to the site
3. **Remote access termination points**—Defines the remote access network's endpoints
4. **Remote access providers**—Defines who manages the remote access network

The two types of remote access networks are as follows:

- **Site-to-site**—Interconnects multiple users at two physical locations
- **User-to-site**—Allows a remote user to access a central site

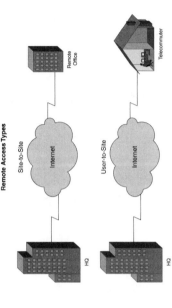

Remote Access Types

Options for remote dialup access include the following:

- **Modem**—Slower speed with moderate cost
- **ISDN**—Moderate speed with moderate cost
- **Cell phone**—Low speed with high cost

Options for remote broadband access include the following:

- **DSL/cable**—Low to high speed with moderate cost
- **Satellite**—Moderate to high speed with high cost

The Point-to-Point Protocol (PPP) is the most common protocol used for connecting user devices to remote termination points. PPP offers several features, such as authentication, callback, multilink support, and link-fragmentation and interleaving. In addition to PPP over a leased line, there are also specifications for PPP over Ethernet (PPPoE) and PPP over ATM (PPPoA).

To appropriately a remote access network's bandwidth, you, as a designer, must gather the following information:

- Number of remote users
- Percentage of users simultaneously accessing the network
- Amount of bandwidth required by each user

You can use the following formula to calculate the total required bandwidth:

Total BW = (Number of Users) * (Percentage of Users Logged In) * (Required BW per User)

Note   To allow for growth, proactively anticipate the number of users that must be supported in the future.

Internet Connectivity Module

The Internet Connectivity module provides Internet access for your internal users and allows Internet users to access resources at your site. Therefore, in addition to functionality, performance, scalability, availability, manageability, and cost effectiveness, security is an important design consideration for traffic coming from the Internet into your network.

Depending on the selected IP addressing scheme, you might use Network Address Translation (NAT) to convert between private internal IP addresses and public external IP addresses. You can choose to deploy one of the following types of NAT:

- **Static NAT**—A one-to-one mapping of private internal IP addresses to public external IP addresses

- **Dynamic NAT**—A dynamic mapping of private internal IP addresses to a pool of public external IP addresses
- **NAT Overloading**—Allows multiple private internal IP addresses to use a single public external IP address by keeping track of Layer 4 port numbers, thereby making each session unique (for example, Port Address Translation [PAT])
- **Overlapping NAT**—Used when private internal IP addresses at one location overlap destination IP addresses at another location

If the site you are connecting to the Internet has a single connection to an ISP, you might choose for the router that connects to the ISP to have a default route pointing to the ISP. This approach alleviates the need for the router to maintain a copy of the full Internet routing table.

However, if you select a multihomed design (that is, the site attaches to more than one ISP) for redundancy or throughput reasons, run BGP on the routers that connect to the ISPs. BGP allows all of your ISPs to advertise your local autonomous system and, in the event that the connection to one of the ISPs fails, your internal users can still access Internet resources, and vice-versa. In a multihomed configuration, your autonomous system could inadvertently become a transit autonomous system, in which traffic flowing across the Internet backbone crosses through your site. Specify AS-path filters to prevent this phenomenon from occurring.

Network Management

Network management systems improve the performance, scalability, and availability of today's networks by providing visibility into the status of network components. CiscoWorks is the Cisco flagship product for network management.

Network Management Goals

The International Organization for Standardization (ISO) formalized a framework for network management known as FCAPS:

- Fault Management
- Configuration Management
- Accounting Management
- Performance Management
- Security Management

Policies and Procedures

Part of network management revolves around developing policies for monitoring and securing the network, escalating a problem that needs more immediate and qualified attention, and alerting users and administrators about network changes.

Procedures detail precise response steps to take in the event of a network problem. Specifically, procedures address the following:

1. "What if" scenarios
2. Step-by-step recovery methods
3. How to notify administrators and users
4. Generating of trouble tickets
5. Documenting the situation for future reference and "post mortem" (that is, after the situation occurred and has been addressed) review

Complete the following six-step process to develop a network management strategy for an enterprise network:

1. Identify the devices to be managed.
2. Identify what information to retrieve from those devices.
3. Specify a measurable goal for network management to ensure that the network management system is performing as expected.
4. Identify what hardware/software components will gather the specified data.
5. Identify thresholds for the criteria being measured.
6. Establish plans of action to handle "what if" scenarios.

Functions of the Network Management Module

The Network Management module typically includes one or more of the following devices/services:

- Authentication server
- Access control server
- Network monitoring server
- IDS director
- Syslog server
- System administration server

The network administrator can access device information via in-band management (that is, using the same communication paths used by production traffic), out-of-band management (that is, using a dedicated communication path that is separate from production traffic), or a terminal server (that is, an out-of-band management approach that allows the administrator to connect to a terminal server and serially access the console ports on the managed devices from there).

Cisco network management strategy involves a simplified, yet secure, web-based approach. Specifically, the Cisco primary network management software product is CiscoWorks.

CiscoWorks

CiscoWorks is not a single application. Rather, it is a collection of network management products that operate in concert to provide a customized network management solution. CiscoWorks is built around the Common Management Foundation (CMF), which provides a web-based, single point of management. CiscoWorks has the ability to "discover" the network via technologies including Cisco Discovery Protocol (CDP) and Simple Network Management Protocol (SNMP).

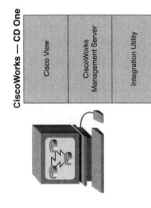

CiscoWorks — CD One

Cisco View

CiscoWorks
Management Server

Integration Utility

CD One, which is the foundational CiscoWorks packet you install, contains the following:

- **CiscoView**—A web-based application that provides status, monitoring, and configuration information for a managed Cisco device
- **CiscoWorks Management Server**—Includes the components that are necessary for launching the CiscoWorks desktop
- **Integration Utility**—Supports integration with third-party network management solutions

In addition to CD One, all CiscoWorks product bundles also include the Resource Manager Essentials (RME) product. The RME includes the following:

- **Inventory Manager**—Provides an inventory of all Cisco devices
- **Configuration Manager**—Maintains a log of configuration changes and has the ability to modify stored configuration changes
- **Software Image Manager**—Streamlines the process of updating the software on multiple Cisco switches and routers
- **Change Audit**—Allows the administrator to view changes made to managed devices
- **Availability Manager**—Displays status information of critical routers and switches
- **Syslog Analyzer**—Filters syslog data to build customizable reports

To assist in LAN management, consider the CiscoWorks LAN Management Solution (LMS), which is a suite of applications that includes the following:

- **Campus Manager**—Enables the administrator to configure, monitor, and maintain a Catalyst-based switched infrastructure with tools including the following:
  - Topology services
  - User tracking
  - Path analysis
  - VLAN port assignment
- **nGenius Real-Time Monitor**—Provides access to real-time monitoring (RMON) and RMON2 information.
- **Device Fault Manager**—Provides the administrator with real-time analysis of Cisco device faults

CiscoWorks — LAN Management Solution (LMS)

Best practices for CiscoWorks LMS include using the RME to archive configurations and software, using the Campus Manager to identify Layer 2 misconfigurations (for example, mismatched VTP domains), and using nGenius to get a feel for the overall health of the network (that is, not just information that a device is "up" or "down").

Just as CiscoWorks has the LMS module for LANs, the CiscoWorks Routed WAN Management Solution (RWAN) for WANs includes the following components:

- **Internetwork Performance Monitor (IPM)**—Sends Service Assurance Agent (SAA) probes into the network to measure network response time and drop characteristics for various traffic types (such as HTTP or Voice over IP)
- **Access Control List (ACL) Manager**—Provides a convenient editor to configure and then distribute access control lists

CiscoWorks — Routed WAN (RWAN) Solution

Network Management Infrastructure

The network management infrastructure's performance can impact the entire network's performance. Therefore, consider the following questions:

- How many management stations are required?
- Will management stations be centralized or distributed?

Best practices for the CiscoWorks RWAN solution include using IPM to monitor response times on critical network services, such as DNS and DHCP. This is possible with IPM because the SAA probes that IPM uses can emulate these, among other traffic types. Also, the ACL Manager should be used to more efficiently standardize and optimize existing and future ACLs.

- Will a hierarchical network management design, similar to the network infrastructure, be used?
- Will the network management network be a separate network or part of the existing network?
- What types of management tools (for example, tools to manage particular network devices or enterprise-wide policy management tools) are required?
- Will NAT And firewall devices block SNMP traffic for security reasons?

Network Management Data Collection

Another important consideration for network management design is to determine the specifics of how data is collected. Consider the following questions as part of your design process:

- Will polling devices create network management traffic, or will events generate network management traffic?
- How much bandwidth should be allocated to support network management traffic across WAN links?
- How will you mitigate the security risks associated with deploying network management protocols such as SNMP and RMON?
- Will you disallow management access to devices via access protocols, such as Telnet and HTTP, for security concerns?
- Will network management traffic be sent in-band (that is, as part of the production network traffic) or out-of-band (that is, outside of the production network traffic)?

Sizing Recommendations

Sizing the network management solution appropriately prevents the network management stations from becoming overloaded, thereby impacting performance. Therefore, consider the following rules-of-thumb when sizing a CiscoWorks-based network management solution:

- A single network management station running the LAN Management Solution supports up to 2000 managed devices or up to 40,000 end-user devices (that is, PCs).
- A management domain containing multiple network management stations can be created, and the various network management stations within the domain can perform different tasks (for example, device fault management, resource management, or campus management).

- When the size of a management domain exceeds 2000, divide the network into multiple management domains. For networks containing fewer than 5000 managed devices, a centralized station should perform resource management.
- While a single instance of CiscoWorks LAN Management Solutions (LMS) or Routed WAN (RWAN) Management Solutions supports up to 2000 devices, a CiscoWorks Resource Manager Essentials (RME) server can manage a maximum of 500 to 1000 network devices, depending on the processing power of the system running the RME software.

High Availability

High Availability Measurement

A system's availability is measured by its uptime during a year. For example, if a device has "five nines" of availability, it is up 99.999 percent of the time. This translates to a maximum of five minutes of downtime per year. If a system has "six nines" of availability (that is, up 99.9999 percent of the time), it is down less than 30 seconds per year.

As a designer, one of your goals is to select components, topologies, and features that maximize network availability, within certain parameters (for example, budget). Do not confuse availability with reliability. For example, a reliable network does not drop many frames; however, an available network is up and operational.

High Availability Design

The availability of a network increases as the network devices' Mean Time To Repair (MTTR) decreases and as the Mean Time Between Failures (MTBF) increases. Therefore, selecting reliable networking devices that are quick to repair is crucial to high-availability design.

Fault-Tolerant Campus Design

Two approaches to designing a fault-tolerant network include the following:

- **Single points of failure**—For example, Layer 3 switches with redundancy built into the devices (for example, redundant supervisor engines)
- **No single points of failure**—For example, multiple paths between multiple Layer 3 switches

An end system (for example, a mission-critical server) can have redundant network interface cards (NICs). The two modes of NIC redundancy are

- **Active-Active**—Both NICs are active at the same time, and they have their own MAC addresses. This makes troubleshooting more complex, while giving you slightly better performance than the Active-Standby approach.
- **Active-Standby**—Only one NIC is active at any time. This approach allows the client to appear to have a single MAC address and IP address, even in the event of an NIC failure.

Layer 3 Redundancy

End systems not running a routing protocol point to a default gateway. The default gateway is traditionally the IP address of a router on the local subnet. However, if the default gateway router fails, the end systems cannot leave their subnet. Two approaches to Layer 3 redundancy include: HSRP and VRRP. With both of these technologies, more than one router can service the MAC address and the default gateway's IP address. Therefore, if a default gateway router goes down, another router can take over, still servicing the same MAC and IP addresses.

- **HSRP** is a Cisco-proprietary approach to Layer 3 redundancy.
- **VRRP** is a standards-based approach to Layer 3 redundancy.

Layer 3 redundancy is also achieved by placing multiple links between devices and selecting a routing protocol that load balances over the links. EtherChannel is another way of load balancing across multiple links. With EtherChannel, you can define up to eight physical links that are logically bundled together so that the bundle appears as a single link to the route processor.

Spanning Tree Protocol Redundancy

The IEEE 802.1D standard is the legacy approach to Layer 2 loop avoidance. By default, in the event of a link failure, 802.1D takes 50 seconds to converge. Cisco added proprietary enhancements to speed up the convergence time. These Cisco-proprietary STP enhancements include:

- **PortFast**—Used on ports that connect to end stations
- **UplinkFast**—Used on building access switches
- **BackboneFast**—Used on all switches in the topology

Each VLAN can run its own instance of STP. This Per-VLAN STP approach allows different VLANs to have different Root Bridges. However, with the Cisco Per-VLAN STP, every VLAN must run its own instance of STP; this can place unnecessary overhead on the switches.

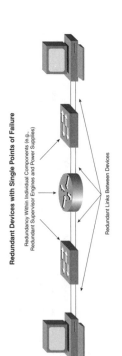

Redundant Devices with Single Points of Failure

Redundancy Within Individual Components (e.g.,
Redundant Supervisor Engines and Power Supplies)

Redundant Links Between Devices

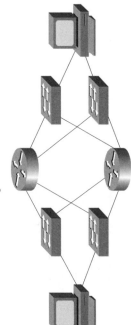

No Single Points of Failure

- Redundant links and redundant devices from end-to-end create a network with no single points of failure.
- Any single link or any single router or switch could fail, without loosing end-to-end connectivity.

Hardware Redundancy

Having redundant route processors in the chassis improves the chassis' reliability. For example, if a Layer 3 Catalyst switch has two route processors, one of the route processors is active, and the other route processor is in standby (that is, not processing packets). If the primary route processor fails, the standby route processor takes over switch operations.

The new IEEE 802.1w and 802.1s protocols achieve the best of both worlds. IEEE 802.1w (that is, Rapid Spanning Tree Protocol) dramatically reduces convergence times in the event of a failure. IEEE 802.1s (that is, Multiple Spanning Tree) allows you to create a set of STP instances. Then, you can assign VLANs to appropriate STP instances. This negates the Per-VLAN STP requirement that each VLAN runs its own instance of STP.

Design Considerations for High Availability Networks

When designing networks for high availability, answer the following questions:

- Where will module and chassis redundancy be used?
- What software redundancy features are appropriate?
- What protocol characteristics affect design requirements?
- What high availability features are required of service provider circuits?
- What redundancy features should be used to provide power to the switch and to maintain environmental conditions?

Module redundancy provides redundancy within a chassis by allowing one module take over in the event that a primary module fails.

Chassis redundancy provides redundancy by having more than one chassis, thus providing a path from the source to destination even in the event of a chassis or link failure.

High Availability Best Practices

Following are five best practices for designing high availability networks:

1. Examine technical goals.
2. Identify the budget to fund high availability features.
3. Categorize business applications into profiles.
4. Establish performance standards for high availability solutions.
5. Define how to manage and measure the high availability solution.

Server Farm High Availability Design

The server farm module contains mission-critical devices and therefore requires high-available design features. Best practices for server farm high availability design include the following:

- Include redundant components in networking devices.
- Provide redundant paths between devices.
- Optionally, use two NICs in the servers (that is, dual homing).

Enterprise Edge High Availability Design

The Enterprise Edge functional area is the transit area between the Campus Infrastructure and the Service Provider Edge. Therefore, a highly available design is critical. Consider the following when designing the Enterprise Edge:

- Obtain a signed Service Level Agreement (SLA) from your service provider.
- Use redundant links (for example, dual PVCs).
- Load balance traffic across redundant links.
- If the redundant links have different speeds, use policy-based routing (PBR) to send different traffic types down different links.
- Choose a routing protocol such as EIGRP or OSPF to minimize Layer 3 convergence.

Network Security

Security Risks

Over the past two decades, the technical knowledge required for a potential hacker to compromise a system decreased as the sophistication of hacker tools increased. Common security threats include the following:

- **Loss of privacy**—For example, obtaining another user's password via eavesdropping
- **Data theft**—For example, making a copy of a private document
- **Impersonation**—For example, gaining access to restricted resources by pretending to be a different user
- **Loss of integrity**—For example, manipulating data in transit

Security Policy

A foundational requirement for designing a secure network is the authoring of a security policy. A security policy defines the assets that are to be protected, the affected users, when a user is allowed to perform an action, how the policy is enforced, the result of a policy violation, how violations are detected, and what actions to perform in the event of a policy violation.

The following are the components of a security policy:

- **Acceptable use policy**—How the network is to be used
- **Identification and authentication policy**—How a user's identity is verified
- **Internet use policy**—What actions are valid uses of the Internet

- **Campus access policy**—When a user can access campus resources from inside the campus
- **Remote access policy**—When a user can access campus resources from a remote location

Security Process

Designing a network's security is a continuous process and is represented by the following steps:

- **Secure**—Apply security solutions
- **Monitor**—Observe the security solutions' operation
- **Test**—Verify the network's integrity by testing various methods of compromising the network
- **Improve**—Repeat this process again based on the results of the testing

Not all network resources require the same degree of protection. Therefore, as part of the design process, identify a risk level (that is, low, medium, or high) associated with a particular resource (such as a printer or a server) being breached. Also, create different privilege levels for different classes of users (for example, administrators, partners, or users).

Security Keys

The security solutions Cisco offers can be categorized into the following five categories:

1. **Secure connectivity**—Protecting information from eavesdropping
2. **Perimeter security**—Making sure that only authorized users access network resources
3. **Intrusion protection**—Uses technologies such as vulnerability scanners to test the network's integrity
4. **Identity**—Uses access servers, such as the Cisco Secure Access Control Server (ACS), to authenticate and authorize users
5. **Security management**—Uses tools to analyze and manage security solutions on an enterprise-wide basis, perhaps via a GUI

Security Attacks and Mitigations

Several mitigations exist for security attacks. However, to select the appropriate response, you must understand more about the type of attack against which you are protecting. Table 1 lists attack types and their appropriate mitigations.

Table 1

Type of Attack	Mitigations
Packet sniffers (capture network traffic)	Authentication Using switches instead of hubs Anti-sniffer tools Cryptography
IP spoofing (where a hacker appears to be coming from a trusted device)	Access control RFC 2827 filtering (prevents your network from being the source of a denial of service [DoS] attack) Authentication
Denial of service (which makes a service unavailable)	Anti-spoof features Anti-DoS features Rate-limiting
Password attacks (repeated attempts to determine the password for a user account)	One-Time Password (OTP) Cryptographic authentication "Strong" passwords
Man-in-the-middle attacks (the interception of packets)	Cryptography
Application layer attacks (where an application vulnerability is exploited)	System administration best practices Keeping patches current Intrusion Detection Systems
Network reconnaissance (gathering information about a network, perhaps through the use of applications)	Port scans to identify unnecessary open ports Intrusion Detection Systems
Trust exploitation (taking advantage of a configured trust relationship)	Never completely trust systems outside of the firewall Only trust specific protocols Authenticate usage using more than just IP addresses

Type of Attack	Mitigations
Port redirection (uses a compromised system to pass through a firewall)	Appropriate trust models Host-based Intrusion Detection Systems
Unauthorized Access (users accessing network resources for which they are not authorized)	Access control lists (ACLs) on routers, or firewalls to limit available ports to which unauthorized users can attach
Virus and Trojan horse (applications that are potentially destructive and that take advantage of workstation vulnerabilities)	Anti-virus software

Firewall Considerations

You must make both business and technical decisions when designing a firewall into your security solution. For example, business decisions include determining how "strict" to configure the firewall, how to configure the firewall to support the documented security policy, and how network monitoring is performed. Technical decisions include, for example, deciding at what layer of the OSI Reference Model to monitor, determining if users send data directly out of the network or if they use a proxy, selecting either a hardware-based firewall (for example, PIX) or a router running the IOS Firewall feature set.

Often, you want to allow outside users to access your site's resources, but you do not want to allow them all the way into your site. You can accomplish this with a perimeter LAN, which is an area of the network that sits between the outside network and the inside network.

When selecting a firewall, consider a PIX Firewall or an IOS Firewall. A PIX Firewall is a dedicated firewall appliance and therefore has little, if any impact on network performance. An IOS Firewall is simply a Cisco router that runs the IOS Firewall feature set. The IOS Firewall feature set is appropriate for a personal firewall or for small networks.

Intrusion Detection System Considerations

An Intrusion Detection System (IDS) examines traffic; an IDS can respond if it recognizes the signature of a "well-known" attack. For example, the IDS might send an alarm, send a TCP Reset, or block traffic coming from the offending device.

Host-based IDS is software that resides on individual hosts and that can protect application software. Network-based IDS is a hardware device (such as a stand-alone appliance or a module in a Catalyst switch) that compares packets against a database of well-known attack signatures.

IDS design best practices include the following:

- Configuring the IDS to make the data relevant
- Optimizing the configuration to reduce "false positives"
- Placing IDS resources in close proximity to critical devices

AAA

An Authentication, Authorization, and Accounting (AAA) device validates a user's credentials, determines what resources the user can access, and logs activity. Various protocols are available for performing these types of functions:

- **RADIUS**—Allows Cisco devices to send authentication requests to a RADIUS server for authentication, but only encrypts the access-request packet from the client to the server
- **TACACS+**—Similar to RADIUS, except that all traffic sent between the Cisco device and the TACACS+ server is encrypted
- **Kerberos**—Uses the concept of a trusted third party (that is, Key Distribution Center) that hands out "tickets" that are used instead of a username and password combination
- **Public Key Infrastructure (PKI)**—Uses the concept of a certificate authority, with which all devices wishing to communicate with each other have already registered

IPSec

IP Security (IPSec) is a process for encrypting and protecting packets at Layer 3. IPSec's four primary goals are as follows:

- **Data confidentiality**—Scrambles data so eavesdroppers cannot interpret it
- **Data integrity**—Uses hashing algorithms to make sure that data was not manipulated
- **Data origin authentication**—Verifies that the packet came from the person from whom you think it came
- **Anti-replay**—Prevents packets captured by a network sniffer from being replayed to spoof the entry of valid credentials

IPSec uses two secure tunnels established between peers. The first tunnel is called the IKE Phase I tunnel. This Internet Key Exchange (IKE) phase automates the process of negotiating many of the details of the security association between two devices. The

IKE Phase II tunnel is brought up to support IPSec services. The IKE Phase II tunnel negotiates its parameters within the protection of the IKE Phase I tunnel.

IPSec Tunnel

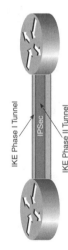

IKE Phase I Tunnel

IPSec

IKE Phase II Tunnel

The IKE Phase I tunnel negotiates the details of the security association between two devices. The IKE Phase II tunnel is brought up, within the protection of the IKE Phase I tunnel, to support IPSec services.

Another protocol IPSec uses is Authentication Header (AH), which runs a hashing algorithm between the IP header and the remainder of the payload. The packet can calculate its own hash and, if the two values match, the packet has not been manipulated.

Similar to AH, the Encapsulating Security Payload (ESP) can check each packet's integrity. However, unlike AH, which has issues coexisting with NAT, ESP is compatible with Network Address Translation (NAT).

Securing Network Components

The following are examples of best practice recommendations for securing routers, switches, hosts, networks, and applications:

- **Routers**
  - Restrict Telnet access
  - Restrict SNMP access
  - Disable unnecessary services
  - Carry out an appropriate amount of logging
  - Authenticate routing protocol updates
  - Use secure commands and control
- **Switches**
  - Use the security procedures used on routers
  - Set the trunking mode to "off" for non-trunking interfaces
  - Place all trunk interfaces in an unused VLAN
  - Disable unused interfaces
  - Separate devices using VLANs, and perhaps private VLANs
- **Hosts**
  - Maintain current patches on operating systems
  - Ensure that patches do not negatively impact other system components
  - Test the patches on non-production systems before deploying patches on production systems
- **Networks**
  - Limit traffic rates
  - Identify undesirable traffic
  - Prevent IP spoofing by filtering based on RFC 1918
  - Prevent your site from being used for a distributed denial of service (DDoS) attack by filtering based on RFC 2817
- **Applications**
  - Maintain current application patches
  - Verify that applications do not introduce additional security risks

SAFE

The main goal of the Cisco Secure Architecture For Enterprise (SAFE) blueprint is to provide best practice information for designing and implementing secure networks. The SAFE architecture categorizes devices and security threats into Enterprise Composite Network Model modules. For a comprehensive examination of the SAFE blueprint, visit the following link: http://www.cisco.com/en/US/netsol/ns110/ns170/ns171/ns128/networking_solutions_white_paper09186a008009_c8b6.shtml

Quality of Service

QoS Design Requirements

Voice, video, and data all travel over today's converged networks. Some of these traffic types (for example, Voice over IP) need better treatment (higher priority) than other types of traffic (for example, FTP). Fortunately, Cisco offers a suite of quality of service (QoS) tools for providing special treatment for special traffic.

In the absence of QoS, traffic might suffer from one or more of the following symptoms:

- **Delay (latency)**—Excessive time required for a packet to traverse the network
- **Delay variation (jitter)**—The uneven arrival of packets, which can the listener can interpret as dropped voice packets in the case of Voice over IP
- **Packet loss**—Dropping packets; this is especially problematic for UDP traffic (for example, Voice over IP), which does not retransmit dropped packets

IntServ and DiffServ

There are two categories of QoS tools: Integrated Services (IntServ) and Differentiated Services (DiffServ). Integrated Services provides QoS by guaranteeing treatment to a particular traffic flow. A commonly used IntServ tool is Resource Reservation Protocol (RSVP).

As its name suggests, DiffServ differentiates (that is, classifies) between different types of traffic and provides different service levels based on those distinctions. Rather than forcing each network device to classify traffic, DiffServ can mark packets with a particular priority marking that other network devices can reference.

A common type of packet marking is Differentiated Services Code Point (DSCP), which uses the six left-most bits in an IPv4 header's ToS byte. With six bits at its disposal, up to 64 DSCP values (0 to 63) can be assigned to various classes of traffic. Simply marking a packet does not change its operation, unless QoS tools are enabled that can reference that marking. Fortunately, there are multiple QoS tools that can make decisions based on these markings.

Layer 3 Packet Markings

Most QoS tools can be placed into one of the following categories:

- Classification and marking
- Congestion avoidance
- Congestion management
- Traffic conditioning
- Signaling
- Link efficiency mechanisms

Classification and Marking

When configuring QoS, decide which network devices you "trust" to make markings. These devices should be as close to the source as possible. For example, you might select a Cisco IP phone as the trust boundary.

After you decide on a trust boundary, configure your edge devices to classify traffic into classes. For example, you could have a Voice over IP (VoIP) class, a database class, an FTP class, a video class, and a default class.

When the traffic is categorized into traffic classes, mark the various traffic classes with DSCP markings to prevent other network devices from having to reclassify the traffic. Instead, these other devices can simply reference the DSCP markings. However, as mentioned earlier, marking by itself does not alter the traffic's behavior.

Congestion Avoidance

The purpose of congestion avoidance is to prevent an interface's output queue from filling to capacity; if a queue is completely full, all newly arriving packets are discarded. Some of those packets might be high priority, and some might be low priority. However, if the queue is full, there is no room for any packet.

With a congestion avoidance tool, drop thresholds are defined for various markings (for example, DSCP markings). Therefore, as a queue begins to fill, lower priority packets are dropped more aggressively than higher priority packets, thus preventing the queue from filling to capacity. Cisco congestion avoidance tool of choice is Weighted Random Early Detection (WRED).

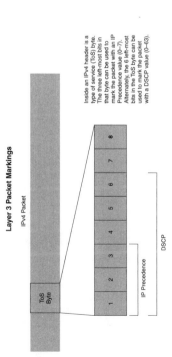

IPv4 Packet

ToS Byte

1 2 3 4 5 6 7 8

IP Precedence

DSCP

Inside an IPv4 header is a type of service (ToS) byte. The three left-most bits in that byte can be used to mark the packet with an IP Precedence value (0–7). Alternately, the 6 left-most bits in the ToS byte can be used to mark the packet with a DSCP value (0–63).

Weighted Random Early Detection (WRED)

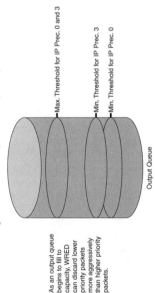

As an output queue begins to fill to capacity, WRED can discard lower priority packets more aggressively than higher priority packets.

Max. Threshold for IP Prec. 0 and 3

Min. Threshold for IP Prec. 3

Min. Threshold for IP Prec. 0

Output Queue

Congestion Management

Congestion management tools are queuing tools that decide how packets are placed in and forwarded out of an interface's output queue. Several queuing tools are available in the IOS:

- **First-in, first-out (FIFO)**—The default queuing mechanism on high-speed interfaces, which does not reorder packets.

- **Weighted fair queuing (WFQ)**—The default queuing mechanism on low-speed interfaces that bases forwarding decisions on a packet's size and priority marking.

- **Low latency queuing (LLQ)**—The preferred queuing method for voice and video traffic, where traffic can be classified in up to 64 different classes, with different amounts of bandwidth given to each class, and including the ability to give priority treatment to one or more classes.

- **Priority queuing (PQ)**—A legacy queuing approach with four queues; higher priority queues must be emptied before forwarding traffic from any lower priority queues.

- **Frame Relay PVC interface priority queuing**—A legacy queuing approach in which frames are placed into queues based on their DLCI.

- **Custom queuing (CQ)**—A legacy queuing approach that services up to sixteen queues in a round-robin fashion, emptying a specified number of bytes from each queue during each round-robin cycle.

- **Class-based weighted fair queuing (CB-WFQ)**—Similar to LLQ, except that it does not have a priority queuing mechanism.

- **IP RTP priority**—A legacy queuing approach for voice traffic that placed a range

Traffic Conditioning

While some of the congestion management techniques can guarantee bandwidth amounts, you might want to limit bandwidth usage in some situations. For example, you might want to prevent oversubscription of a link. There are two categories of traffic conditioning:

- **Policing**—Limits traffic rates, with excess traffic being dropped
- **Shaping**—Limits traffic rates, with excess traffic being delayed

As previously mentioned, shaping buffers excess traffic, while policing drops excess traffic. These characteristics suggest that policing is more appropriate on high-speed interfaces, while shaping is more appropriate on low-speed interfaces.

Signaling

The IntServ model uses signaling to allow an application to reserve bandwidth for its duration. RSVP is the primary QoS signaling protocol. One of the main signaling characteristics to consider is that it is performed end-to-end.

Link Efficiency Mechanisms

Link efficiency mechanisms help make the most of limited bandwidth WAN links. Two link efficiency mechanisms include the following:

- **LFI**—Link Fragmentation and Interleaving takes large payloads, fragments them, and interleaves smaller packets among the fragments to reduce serialization delay for latency-sensitive traffic (for use on link speeds less than 768 kbps)

- **CRTP**—RTP Header Compression compresses a 40-byte VoIP header down to approximately 2 to 4 bytes (for use on link speeds lower than 2 Mbps)

QoS Category	QoS Tools
Classification and Marking	ACLs, NBAR, PBR, CoS, IP Precedence, and DSCP
Congestion Avoidance	WRED and FRED
Congestion Management	CB-WFQ, LLQ, CQ, PQ, WFQ, IP RTP Priority
Traffic Conditioning	CB-Policing, CB-Shaping, CAR, GTS, and Frame Relay Traffic Shaping
Signaling	RSVP

QoS Design

Ask the following questions when designing QoS solutions:

- What problems must the QoS tools solve?
- Will the IntServ or DiffServ model be used?
- How should the problem be solved?
- How do different solutions compare in terms of performance and cost?

The following are best practices for data, voice, and video QoS design:

- Data
  - Classify data packets into no more than four classes
- Voice
  - Ensure that one-way delay does not exceed 150 ms
  - Provision sufficient network bandwidth to accommodate the addition of voice traffic, including overhead
- Video
  - Ensure that one-way delay does not exceed 150-200 ms
  - Guarantee enough bandwidth to accommodate the video stream plus 20 percent

The following are QoS requirements for building-access switches:

- Support multiple VLANs
- Manipulate markings provided by end-user systems
- Create a trust boundary close to the source

The following are QoS requirements for the building distribution switches:

- The switches must be QoS-enabled.
- Remark Layer 2 QoS markings (class of service) to Layer 3 QoS markings (for example, DSCP)
- Configure ports to trust appropriate QoS markings (e.g., CoS or DSCP)

The following are QoS recommendations for the campus backbone switches:

- Configure high-speed queuing (for example, LLQ)
- Configure congestion avoidance (for example, WRED)

IP Multicasting

Importance of IP Multicast

Consider a video stream that must be sent to multiple recipients in a company. One approach is to unicast the traffic. The source server sends a copy of each packet to each receiver. Obviously, this approach has serious scalability limitations.

With unicast transmission, a separate copy of every packet must be sent to each receiver.

An alternate approach is to broadcast the video stream so the source server only has to send each packet once. However, in that scenario, everyone in the network receives the packet, even if they do not want it.

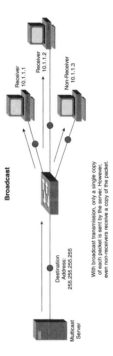

With broadcast transmission, only a single copy of each packet is sent by the server. However, even non-receivers receive a copy of the packet.

IP multicast technologies provide the best of both worlds. With IP multicast, the source server only sends one copy of each packet, and the packets are only sent to intended recipients.

Reverse Path Forwarding (RPF) Check

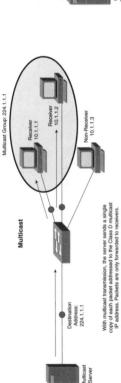

The RPF check compares incoming packets with the unicast routing table to determine if a packet is arriving on the correct interface.

Group Membership/Distribution Trees

Only members of a multicast group receive packets that are destined for that group. However, the sender does not have to be a member of the group.

Multicast traffic flows from a source to a destination over a "distribution tree," which is a loop-free path. The two types of distribution trees are as follows:

- **Source Distribution Tree**—Creates an optimal path between each source router and each last-hop router (that is, a router connected to a receiver) at the expense of increased memory usage
- **Shared Distribution Tree**—Creates a shared tree from a central "rendezvous point" router to all last-hop routers, creating source distribution created from all sources to the rendezvous point at the expense of increased delay

---

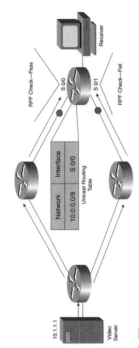

Multicast

With multicast transmission, the server sends a single copy of each packet addressed to the Class D multicast IP address. Packets are only forwarded to receivers.

Specifically, receivers join a multicast group that is denoted by a Class D IP address (in the range of 224.0.0.0 through 239.255.255.255). The source sends traffic to the Class D address, and packets are only forwarded to intended stations through switch and router protocols. These multicast packets are sent via UDP (best effort); therefore, congestion avoidance mechanisms such as WRED, which causes TCP flows to go into TCP slow start, are not effective for multicast. As you complete your multicast design, be aware of the potential for duplicate packets to be received and for packets to arrive out of order.

Multicast Forwarding

To combat the issue of receiving duplicate packets, Cisco routers perform a Reverse Path Forwarding (RPF). Check to determine whether a multicast packet is entering a router on the correct interface. An RPF Check examines the source address of an incoming packet and checks it against the router's unicast routing table to see what interface should be used to return to the source network. If the incoming multicast packet is using that interface, the RPF check passes, and the packet is forwarded. If the multicast packet is coming in on a different interface, the RPF check fails, and the packet is discarded.

The Protocol Independent Multicast (PIM) protocol is a router-to-router protocol that Cisco routers use to achieve a loop-free topology. The two types of PIM are

- **PIM Dense Mode (DM)**
  - Floods multicast traffic over all links
  - Requires routers that do not want the multicast packets to send a "prune" message, which prevents multicast packets from being sent to those routers (*Note:* This flood and prune behavior repeats every three minutes.)
  - Uses the Source Distribution Tree approach, which requires additional memory
  - Useful for small pilot networks
- **PIM Sparse Mode (SM)**
  - Allows routers to explicitly request to join a tree
  - Avoids PIM-DM's flood and prune behavior
  - Uses the Shared Distribution Tree approach
  - Supports "SPT (Shortest Path Tree) Switchover," which allows receiver routers to form a Shortest Path Tree with the source routers immediately after the receiving routers join the shared tree, thus creating optimal pathing
  - Appropriate for production networks with a sparse or dense distribution of receivers

Control Mechanisms

When a Layer 2 switch receives a multicast frame on an interface, the switch floods the frame out all other interfaces by default. To prevent this behavior, the switch must know what interfaces are connected to receivers for specific multicast groups. Two approaches for training the switch include

- **CGMP (Cisco Group Management Protocol)**—A Cisco-proprietary approach that is used on lower-end switches and allows a Cisco router to inform a Cisco switch which of its interfaces are connected to multicast receivers for specific multicast groups
- **IGMP snooping**—Used on higher-end switches; allows a switch to autonomously determine which interfaces are connected to receivers for specific multicast groups by eavesdropping on the IGMP traffic that is exchanged between clients and routers

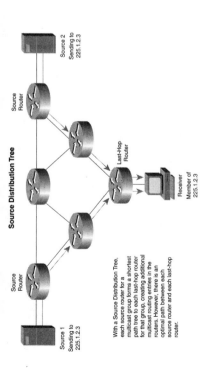

Source Distribution Tree

Source 1 Sending to 225.1.2.3

Source 2 Sending to 225.1.2.3

Source Router

Source Router

Last-Hop Router

Receiver Member of 225.1.2.3

With a Source Distribution Tree, each source router for a multicast group forms a shortest path tree to each last-hop router for that group, creating additional multicast routing entries in the routers. However, there is an optimal path between each source router and each last-hop router.

Shared Distribution Tree

Source 1 Sending to 225.1.2.3

Source 2 Sending to 225.1.2.3

Source Router

Source Router

Rendezvous Point (RP)

Last-Hop Router

Receiver Member of 225.1.2.3

With a Shared Distribution Tree, each source router for a multicast group forms a shortest path tree to the RP. The RP then sends the multicast data to the last-hop routers. The Shared Distribution Tree approach results in fewer routing entries in the routers. However, suboptimal paths often result.

The following are inter-domain multicast routing protocols:

- Border Gateway Multicast Protocol (BGMP)—A protocol that is still in development; its goal is to become a multicast routing protocol that can scale to the Internet
- Multicast BGP (MBGP)—An extension of BGP that allows autonomous systems to exchange multicast RPF information as MBGP multicast Network Layer Reachability Information (NLRI)
- Multicast Source Discovery Protocol (MSDP)—Works with PIM-SM to allows rendezvous points (RPs) in one domain to announce their sources to another domain

The protocol used between clients (for example, PCs) and routers to let routers know which of their interfaces have multicast receivers attached is IGMP. Currently, there are three versions of IGMP:

- IGMP Version 1—When a PC wants to join a multicast group, it sends an IGMP Report to the router to let the router know that it wants to receive traffic for a specific group. By default, the router sends an IGMP Query every 60 seconds to determine whether the PC still wants to belong to the group. There can be up to a 3-minute delay before the time the router realizes that the receiver left the group.
- IGMP Version 2—Similar to IGMP Version 1, except that IGMP Version 2 can send queries to a specific group, and it supports a "leave" message. Specifically, a receiver can proactively send a leave message when it no longer wishes to participate in a multicast group, thereby allowing the router to prune its interface earlier.
- IGMP Version 3—IGMP Version 3 supports Source-Specific Multicast (SSM), which allows multiple source servers (that contain different content) to send traffic to the same multicast group. The receivers can then request not only to receive traffic destined for a specific group, but to also receive traffic from specific servers.

IP Multicast Networks

Perform the following steps when designing a multicast solution:

- Identify the source of the multicast traffic
- Identify which receivers can receive traffic for the group
- Specify how receivers join the group
- Select PIM-DM or PIM-SM as the router-to-router multicast protocol
- If PIM-SM is used, identify one or more rendezvous points (RPs)
- Provision bandwidth on links to support multicast traffic

For small campus design, use IGMP snooping on switches that support it, and use CGMP on switches that do not support IGMP snooping. Place RPs in the building distribution module, or in the campus backbone if you are using a collapsed backbone (that is, if the building distribution and the campus backbone are one in the same). For a large campus design, use IGMP snooping on building access switches and place RPs throughout the network to give different RPs responsibility for different ranges of multicast addresses.

For WAN design, place RPs as close to the multicast source as possible. Use CGMP or IGMP snooping on switches. Also, on the WAN access router, filter out multicast traffic that you do not wish to enter the WAN.

Other design best practices include the following:

- Use group multicast address ranges based on bandwidth requirements to facilitate the filtering of high-bandwidth traffic entering low-bandwidth links.
- For security purposes, use access control lists (ACLs) to restrict which sources can send registrations to an RP, and which devices can act as RPs.

VPNs

The Need for VPNs

Virtual Private Networks (VPNs) support secure communication between network locations. The two primary categories of VPNs are

- Site-to-site—Interconnects two sites, as an alternative to a leased line, at a reduced cost
- Remote access—Interconnects a remote user with a site, as an alternative to dialup or ISDN connectivity, at a reduced cost

These technologies can be combined.

VPN Tunneling

Tunneling is the process of sending one protocol encapsulated inside of another protocol. Site-to-site VPNs typically use Generic Router Encapsulation (GRE) for tunneling. GRE is appropriate when multicast, broadcast, and non-IP packets must pass through the tunnel. However, if you are only tunneling unicast IP packets, IPSec is sufficient.

VPN Security

IPSec can verify the integrity of your data and encrypt the data that is traversing the tunnel. However, VPNs must also authenticate users to prevent inappropriate users from establishing a VPN with your network.

VPN authentication can use client software, or you can choose an authentication server (for example, a RADIUS server) for enhanced authentication. Public Key Infrastructure (PKI) is another option for authenticating remote access users.

Data traveling over your VPN must also needs be encrypted so it cannot be read if it is intercepted. 3DES (Triple Data Encryption Standard) is a common encryption algorithm. Either a router or a dedicated VPN concentrator can perform VPN termination. A design best practice is to consider using a router for less than 70 site-to-site tunnels, and a VPN concentrator for 70 or more site-to-site tunnels.

When selecting a VPN management solution, consider the following characteristics of a good management solution:

- Easy to configure
- Reconfiguration performed dynamically
- Robust configuration options
- Monitoring capabilities and the ability to send alerts before a problem occurs
- Ability to simultaneously monitor multiple devices

CiscoWorks has such a module available for the configuration, monitoring, and troubleshooting of VPNs. For this module, the CiscoWorks VPN/Security Management Solution includes the following modules:

- **VPN Monitor**—Monitors IPSec sessions on routers and concentrators
- **Cisco IDS Host Sensor**—Monitors security threats to critical servers
- **Cisco Secure Policy Manager (CSPM)**—Manages IDS, IOS, and PIX devices and can report alerts about intrusions
- **Resource Manager Essentials (RME)**—Supports software distribution
- **CiscoView**—Graphically displays status information and allows you to configure a network element

Site-to-Site Designs

Site-to-site VPNs interconnect networks at fixed locations. The following are some of the primary characteristics of a site-to-site VPN:

- Can have a hub-and-spoke or a full-mesh topology
- Uses tunneling
- Uses routing protocols to train routers to reach routers at the remote sites
- Carries data, voice, and video

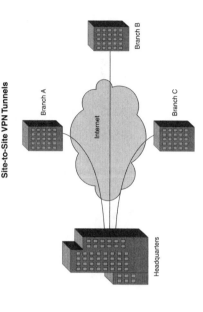

Site-to-Site VPN Tunnels

Site-to-site VPN tunnels typically use GRE tunnels between remote office routers and the main corporate VPN termination device. Data in the GRE tunnel is usually protected via IPSec.

The key components of a site-to-site VPN include the following:

- Cisco head-end VPN routers
- Cisco VPN access routers
- IPSec and GRE tunnels
- Internet access

Site-to-site VPNs often replace private WAN connections. Although a private WAN is considered more secure and has the advantage of being self-managed, it does not scale well. Conversely, site-to-site VPNs can be configured in a redundant topology and are less expensive.

The four primary steps to site-to-site VPN design are

1. Characterize the application demands for the VPN.
2. Select a VPN topology between sites.
3. Add redundant connections.
4. Select a router for the head-end based on anticipated VPN usage.

When selecting a VPN topology, a hub-and-spoke topology might be appropriate when multiple remote offices connect back to central or regional sites, and when most packets are traveling from the remote sites to central or regional sites.

A full-mesh of VPN interconnections adds redundancy to a design and supports the need for frequent communication between remote sites. However, a full-mesh design has scalability limitations.

A compromise between hub-and-spoke and full-mesh is a hierarchical VPN topology. With a hierarchical topology, core sites are interconnected by a full-mesh, with other sites connecting back to the core using a hub-and-spoke design.

For redundancy purposes, you can deploy two tunnels between sites, connecting to different head-end routers. In such a configuration, the sites still have connectivity, even in the event of a tunnel failure or a head-end failure. Routing can be configured so one of these two tunnels functions as the primary tunnel, and the other tunnel functions as a secondary tunnel if the primary tunnel fails.

Challenge of Fragmentation

IPSec makes packets larger by adding additional header information. Similarly, an additional header is added to a packet by a GRE tunnel. If the packet size grows beyond an interface's Maximum Transmission Unit (MTU), the packet is fragmented. To avoid this issue, you can statically specify an MTU size of 1400 bytes. Even after IPSec or GRE header information is added to a 1400-byte frame, its size is still smaller than the default interface MTU of 1500 bytes. IP MTU Discovery, which allows MTU negotiation between VPN devices, is another option.

IPSec VPN Modes

There are two modes of running IPSec over VPNs:

- **Tunnel mode**—Encrypts each packet's header and payload
- **Transport mode**—Only encrypts data

In the Transport mode, GRE does the tunneling. Therefore, the packet does not have as much overhead.

Remote Access Designs

A remote access VPN allows mobile remote users to securely access corporate network resources using DSL, cable-modem, or dialup technology. Typical tunneling protocols used include

- IPSec
- GRE
- L2TP

If you are using a VPN concentrator, place it behind at least one router to avoid direct exposure to the public Internet. Additionally, you might want to protect the concentrator with a firewall or have VPN users authenticate via an AAA server.

Remote Access VPN Tunnels

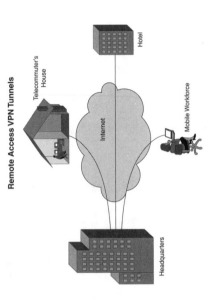

Remote access VPN tunnels typically use IPSec tunnels between a remote user, connecting via an ISP, and the corporate VPN termination device.

Ask the following questions when designing a remote access VPN:

- Is the primary goal remote access?
- What operating systems can be running on client devices?
- What VPN tunneling protocol is appropriate?
- What routing approach (for example, static routes or a specific dynamic routing protocol) is appropriate for the VPN concentrator?
- How should user authentication be performed?
- Should the connection be a persistent connection (up all the time), or should it have a timeout?

Ask the following questions when selecting a firewall for a remote access VPN:

- Does a firewall already exist in the topology?
- Is there an existing security policy that specifies traffic that is permitted to pass through the firewall?
- Are firewall interfaces available to protect the VPN concentrator?

interfaces?

- If only one firewall interface is available, which VPN interface should it protect?

Remote Access Provisioning

Perform the following steps during capacity planning for a remote access VPN:

1. Determine the approximate total number of users.
2. Determine the approximate number of simultaneous users.
3. Identify the bandwidth of the existing ISP connection.
4. Determine the approximate bandwidth required for the ISP connection.
5. Specify how a user connects to the VPN.
6. Estimate future VPN growth.

Remote Access NAT Considerations

If your VPN solution incorporates Network Address Translation (NAT), consider the following:

- Using one-to-one NAT does not create a problem.
- Using Port Address Translation (PAT) can impact IPSec.

Because IPSec runs directly on IP, NAT cannot examine port information in a PAT configuration. One fix is called NAT Traversal, where IPSec peers negotiate an IPSec connection, determine whether NAT is in use, and use a UDP wrapper if it is in use. This UDP wrapper uses port 4500. This fix, sometimes called "packet stuffing," allows only one IPSec connection through a NAT router that runs PAT.

Split-Tunneling

Consider a VPN connection from your home to your corporate headquarters. Do all of your packets—Internet surfing packets, for example—have to go through the corporate network? If not, you can use split-tunneling.

With split-tunneling, only traffic that must flow over the VPN is sent over the VPN. Other traffic is sent unencrypted over the local default gateway—typically your ISP's router.

Split-tunneling offers the benefit of not burdening the corporate head-end with all packets (for example, Internet surfing packets) sent from VPN clients. However, split-tunnels introduce a security risk. If a VPN client downloaded a trojan horse program from the Internet, a hacker might be able to take control of the user's PC, which has a VPN into the corporate network.

Need for Wireless Networks

A wireless LAN (WLAN) can exist in the same building as a wired LAN (that is, overlay the LAN). Such an application is appropriate for users who must work at various locations throughout a building, or for an office space within a building that is expanding. Wireless LANs also offer a solution to two users who must share an office with a single network connection.

In a WLAN, wireless clients communicate with an access point—sometimes called a wireless access point (WAP)—that physically connects to the LAN backbone. However, data rates decrease as the wireless user gets further away from the access point. Additional access points can be added to increase the WLAN's capacity, range, and data rate.

Antenna selection, required speed, power levels, and structural barriers (such as walls) affect the WLAN's coverage area. Therefore, a site survey is required during the design process.

802.11 Standards

The IEEE 802.11 group standardizes protocols for WLANs. The following are the characteristics of three 802.11 standards:

- **IEEE 802.11a**
  - 5 GHz Frequency Band
  - Maximum Data Rates 54 Mbps

- **IEEE 802.11b**
  - 2.4 GHz Frequency Band
  - Maximum Data Rates 11 Mbps

- **IEEE 802.11g**
  - 2.4 GHz Frequency Band
  - Maximum Data Rates 54 Mbps

Note: 802.11g uses the same frequency band as 802.11b and is backwards compatible.

Cisco Wireless Products

Cisco offers both *wireless access points* and *client adapters*. However, optimal placing of an access point can be in a ceiling or in an area of a building where power is not readily accessible. Fortunately, the Cisco wireless access points support inline power, where they can be powered directly over the Ethernet connection from an inline power Catalyst switch.

Wireless Bridge

Office A

Office B

Wireless Bridge

Wireless Bridge

Less than 1 Mile

Remote offices. less than one mile apart and with a line-of-site path between them, can interconnect via wireless bridges.

WLAN Design and Planning

As a design best practice, the maximum number of simultaneous wireless clients associated with a single access point should be in the 10 to 30 range because all wireless clients are using shared bandwidth. You also want to take precautions from having your access point send a signal into an area that should not receive the signal. Obviously, for security purposes, you would not place an Ethernet port in a parking lot; however, that is essentially what you are doing by having an access point's signal extend into the parking lot.

Having multiple access points servicing the same area is an option for supporting a higher user density. However, if multiple access points' signals overlap, the access points must use separate channels. In an IEEE 802.11b environment specifically, the three non-overlapping channels that are defined for use in the same area are channels 1, 6, and 11.

Other WLAN design considerations include the following:

- The requirements for inline power, to power wireless access points
- One or more VLANs dedicated to WLAN traffic
- Using a separate address space for WLAN clients
- Securing wireless communications with EAP, WLAN LAN Extension via IPSec, or WLAN Static WEP.

A Cisco workgroup bridge is appropriate for a cluster of devices in an area without network connectivity. The devices connect via an Ethernet cable to the *workgroup bridge*, which has wireless connectivity back to a wireless access point.

Workgroup Bridge

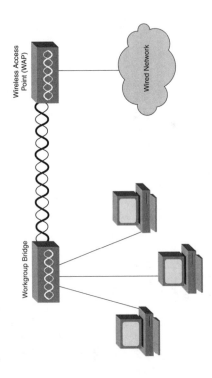

Wireless Access Point (WAP)

Wired Network

Workgroup Bridge

A workgroup bridge contains a hub for interconnecting wired devices, and an antenna for interconnecting with a WAP.

You might have to design connectivity between two buildings. Rather than specifying a leased line, consider a *wireless bridge* if there is a "line of sight" path between the buildings. A wireless bridge achieves greater distance than is possible with standard 802.11b access points by altering 802.11 timing constraints. Depending on the antennas used, wireless bridges have a range of up to a mile.

WLAN Redundancy

To provide high availability to the WLAN, consider the following recommendations:

- High-availability services present in the enterprise network (for example, HSRP and redundant modules within a chassis)

- Backup DHCP and DNS services

- Redundant wireless access points, both operating on the same channel, with one in standby and one active

Mobility, Multicast, and QoS WLAN Support

With workstations no longer tethered with an Ethernet cable, you want to provide for Layer 2 and Layer 3 mobility within the WLAN. Layer 2 mobility is built into the Cisco wireless access points and allows you to move between wireless access points in the same VLAN while maintaining connectivity. However, consider what happens if you move your laptop into an area that is being serviced by a wireless access point in a different VLAN. Consider enabling the Mobile IP IOS feature, which allows devices to keep their IP address regardless of their physical location in the network.

Multicast is a challenge in WLAN. Because all wireless clients use shared bandwidth, each client can see traffic from all other clients. Encryption of multicast traffic is therefore recommended for privacy. However, only a low volume of multicast traffic should be sent over the WLAN because of its impact on every attached wireless client.

Latency-sensitive applications, such as Voice over IP (VoIP), have a challenge in a WLAN environment, because all devices on a WAP use shared bandwidth. However, WAPs can give priority queuing to such traffic as VoIP. As a design best practice, no more than seven IP phones should be associated with a wireless access point.

Designing WLAN Security

To mitigate most security threats in the WLAN, Cisco offers the Cisco Wireless Security Suite of products. Any one solution that is used in isolation is vulnerable. However, you can dramatically increase the WLANs' security by using multiple security tools in concert. Consider the following approaches:

- **WLAN LAN Extension: EAP**—The Extensible Authentication Protocol (EAP) allows a wireless client and a wireless access point to mutually authenticate using a protocol such as 802.1x or RADIUS.

- **WLAN LAN Extension: IPSec**—Just like on a wired network, you can create an IPSec VPN tunnel through the air and encrypt data in that tunnel.

- **WLAN Static WEP**—Static Wired Equivalent Privacy (WEP) uses a key that is manually configured on every wireless client and wireless access point. Static WEP keys are considered one of the weakest approaches to WLAN security. For example, if a laptop configured with the static WEP key is lost or stolen, all of the wireless clients and wireless access points must be manually reconfigured with another static WEP key. Also, a static WEP key can be intercepted and decrypted with a reasonable effort.

Small Office WLAN Design

In a small office environment, WLANs can be used to extend network access to unwired areas of a building that need connectivity. A workgroup bridge might be appropriate for such a design requirement.

For security in a small office environment, consider using EAP for key management. EAP is less intrusive, less expensive, and easier to configure than more robust security solutions.

Enterprise WLAN Design

An enterprise network is likely to have significant amounts of broadcast traffic. Therefore, place WLAN traffic on a separate VLAN.

You must also select an appropriate number of wireless access points, based on the expected number of users. For example, you might want to equip a large conference room with two or three WAPs (using non-overlapping channels) to accommodate a high concentration of users.

For WLAN security in the enterprise network, consider a key management solution, such as EAP, with IPSec VPNs.

WLAN Design for SOHO Environments

Consider the following scenario: A company needs to increase its office space. Space is unavailable in the current building, so a nearby building is selected for the office expansion.

Consider placing multiple WAPs in the new building, perhaps in conjunction with workgroup bridges for a high concentration of devices. This negates the need to run wiring for the new location. Also, they can be interconnected via a wireless bridge if they have a line of sight path between them and they are less than 1 mile apart.

WLAN Design for Enterprise Environments

In small offices or in a telecommuter's home, consider installing an Aironet base station to act as the WAP. This base station would be connected to the broadband connection (for example, a DSL router or a cable modem). Because a telecommuter typically has relatively few devices, a 128-bit static WEP key can be used for security between the wireless client and the base station. For additional security, send traffic to and from the corporate site encrypted over a VPN.

IP Telephony

Components of an IP Telephony Network

Cisco IP telephony solution allows a company to replace their PBX-based telephony solution with a network-based telephony solution that is transparent to users. Key components of an IP telephony network include the following:

- **Call processing engine**—The Cisco CallManager (CCM) is the Cisco call-processing engine. Similar to a legacy PBX, the call processing engine routes voice calls.
- **IP phones**—Cisco IP phones are Ethernet-based phones that can connect to a Catalyst switch. The IP phones can draw power (–48 VDC) from in-line power capable Catalyst switches.
- **Gateways**—A gateway converts from one type of media to another. For example, a PSTN gateway might have an Ethernet interface connecting to the LAN (containing IP phones) and a T1 interface connecting to the PSTN (Public Switched Telephone Network).
- **DSPs**—Digital Signal Processors (DSPs) provide the processing power for tasks such as transcoding (that is, converting between low and high-compression voice encodings) and conference calling (that is, mixing multiple audio streams together).

Cisco CallManager Platform

The Cisco CallManager (CCM) is a software-based call processing engine that runs on the Windows 2000 operating system. The server on which the CCM runs is called an MCS (Media Convergence Server). Although, with current versions of the CCM, the supported number of IP phones per CCM server varies based on the CCM version and MCS platform, the scalability limits specified in these study sheets reflect CCM 3.1 specifications.

CCM Scalability (for CCM Version 3.1)

A single CCM server supports up to 2,500 IP phones. However, multiple CCMs can be logically combined into a CCM cluster. A single CCM cluster supports up to 10,000 phones. For greater scalability, multiple CCM clusters can be interconnected via intercluster trunks. Therefore, there is no practical scalability limitation for a CCM-centric IP telephony network.

CCM Design Models

When designing an IP telephony network, select from one of the four CCM design models:

- **Single-site**—IP phones and CCMs located at a single site
- **Centralized call processing**—IP phones at multiple sites and all CCMs at a single site
- **Distributed call processing**—IP phones and CCMs at multiple sites
- **Clustering over the WAN**—IP phones and CCMs at multiple sites, with all CCMs logically assigned to the same cluster

Gateway Selection

As mentioned previously, gateways support the conversion between different media types. For example, you might need a gateway to pass voice traffic between an analog or digital telephony interface and an Ethernet interface. If your voice network has modems or faxes, the gateways might have to support the transmission of fax and modem tones; this can degrade using high-compression voice coding algorithms (CODECs). Therefore, review the following considerations when selecting a VoIP gateway:

- Voice, fax, and modem support
- Appropriate interface types (for example, analog, digital, or Ethernet)
- Gateway signaling protocol support

VoIP gateways use signaling protocols to set up, maintain, and tear down a call. The following are common gateway protocols:

- **Simple Gateway Control Protocol (SGCP)**—Also known as non-IOS MGCP (Media Gateway Control Protocol). SGCP provides call control between a Cisco CallManager (CCM) and a gateway, such as a Catalyst 6500.
- **Media Gateway Control Protocol (MGCP)**—Acts as a signaling protocol between a CCM and an analog gateway.
- **H.323**—Supports signaling between an IOS router gateway that is configured with dial-peers and a CCM.
- **Session Initiation Protocol (SIP)**—An IETF standard that uses an ASCII-based approach to exchanging call control messages.

As of Cisco CallManager 3.1, CCM does not support SIP. However, the CCM does support both the MGCP and H.323 protocols. MGCP offers easier configuration than H.323, with routers pointing back to the CCM for call routing intelligence. However, H.323 is a more mature protocol with a greater number of supported interfaces.

Transcoding, MTP, and Conferencing

VoIP packets are encoded using a CODEC (Coder Decoder). The G.711 CODEC does not compress voice, and it requires 64 kbps of bandwidth for the voice payload. However, when sending VoIP packets over the WAN, other CODECs can be used to reduce bandwidth requirements. For example, the G.729 CODEC requires 8 kbps of bandwidth for voice payload.

Hardware Digital Signal Processor (DSP) resources are used to convert between G.711 and G.729, for example. The process of converting between low and high-compression CODECs is called Transcoding.

When placing a call on hold or transferring a call, the call must be temporarily terminated on a Media Termination Point (MTP). DSPs provide the hardware resources for an MTP.

DSPs can also be used to support conference calling, in which multiple audio streams are mixed together. Using DSPs to support a conference call is referred to as a hardware conference bridge. However, a CCM can support G.711-only conference calls independently of any DSPs (that is, software conference bridges).

Add-On Applications

Cisco offers a suite of the following add-on voice applications to supplement the CCM:

- **Cisco Customer Response Solution**—Includes such features as interactive voice response
- **Cisco Conference Connection**—A conference server used to facilitate conferences in which all participants dial into a central number
- **Cisco Emergency Responder**—Used to pinpoint the location of 911 callers
- **Cisco IP Contact Center**—Uses Computer Telephony Integration (CTI) to intelligently deliver calls to appropriate contact center agents
- **Cisco IP Phone Productivity Services**—A kit to aid software developers in creating third-party products to integrate with the CCM

- **Cisco Unity**—A converged messaging system designed to consolidate messaging services (for example, the ability to retrieve e-mail over a cell phone via text-to-speech conversion)
- **Cisco Personal Assistant**—An application that works with Unity, allowing users to specify how they can be reached based on calling party information

CCM Clusters

A CCM cluster is a grouping of at least two CCMs that work together and use the same database of information. One of the CCMs in a cluster is the publisher, and the remaining CCMs in that cluster are subscribers. The publisher pushes out a copy of the cluster's database to the subscribers, who have a read-only copy of the database.

With CCM 3.1, cluster sizes ranged from 2 to 8 CCMs. The following are the recommended number of CCM servers to support a specified maximum number of IP phones:

- 2500 IP phones—2 CCMs
- 5000 IP phones—4 CCMs
- 10,000 IP phones—8 CCMs

In addition to registering IP phones and placing calls, the CCM can communicate with other devices types (e.g., an H.323 gateway) and provide services (e.g., conference calling). These extra communication paths and service paths require CCM resources, which are measured in "device weights." The actual device weights vary based on traffic load. The traffic load is measured in Busy Hour Call Attempts (BHCAs). As of CCM 3.1, 5000 was the maximum number of device units supported on a single CCM server.

CCM Design Guidelines

Earlier, you saw the four CCM design models. Now, consider some of the characteristics for each of those models:

- **Single-Site Model**
  - Contains no more than 10,000 phones per cluster
  - Uses the G.711 CODEC for all calls
  - Leverages high availability features in the network infrastructure
  - Has a simplified dial plan
  - Uses MGCP gateways for the PSTN, unless H.323 functions are required

Single-Site CCM Model

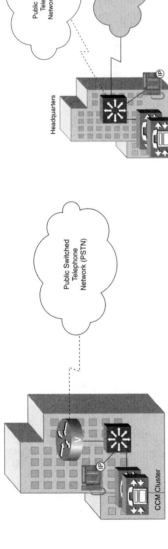

With single-site CCM model, all CCMs and IP phones reside at a single location. The PSTN is used for all calls between the campus and the outside world.

- **Centralized Call Processing Model**
  - Contains no more than 10,000 phones per cluster
  - CCM cluster located at a central site
  - IP phones located at multiple sites
  - Uses DSPs for MTP, conferencing, and transcoding
  - Lower maintenance costs than Distributed Call Processing Model
  - Uses Survivable Remote Site Telephony (SRST) for remote site redundancy
  - Uses WAN bandwidth for call setup
  - Uses MGCP or H.323 at the central location, and H.323 at remote locations

Centralized Call-Processing CCM Model

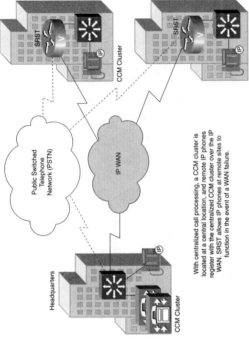

With centralized call processing, a CCM cluster is located at a central location, and remote IP phones register with the centralized CCM cluster over the IP WAN. SRST allows IP phones at remote sites to function in the event of a WAN failure.

- **Distributed Call Processing Model**
  - Can scale to hundreds of sites.
  - Contains multiple sites, each with their own CCM cluster.
  - Contains no more than 10,000 phones per cluster.
  - WAN failure does not affect local site functionality.
  - Uses a gatekeeper to prevent WAN bandwidth oversubscription.

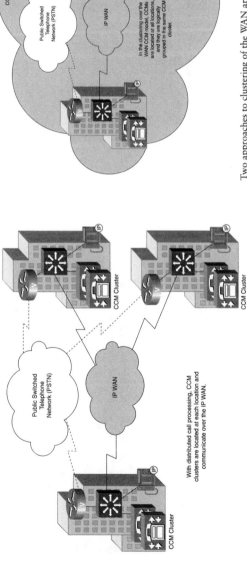

Clustering over the WAN CCM Model

CCM Cluster

Public Switched Telephone Network (PSTN)

IP WAN

In the clustering over the WAN CCM model, CCMs are located at all locations, and they are logically grouped in the same CCM cluster.

Distributed Call-Processing CCM Model

CCM Cluster

CCM Cluster

CCM Cluster

Public Switched Telephone Network (PSTN)

IP WAN

With distributed call processing, CCM clusters are located at each location and communicate over the IP WAN.

- Clustering over the WAN Call Processing Model
  - A cluster composed of CCMs located at multiple sites.
  - Requires 900 kbps of WAN bandwidth for every 10,000 Busy Hour Call Attempts (BHCAs).
  - Requires a maximum round-trip time (RTT) of 40 ms between any two CCMs in the cluster.

Two approaches to clustering of the WAN are Local Failover and Remote Failover:

- **Local Failover**
  - Requires CCM subscriber and backup servers to be located at the same site
  - Appropriate for two to three sites with 2500 to 5000 phones per site
- **Remote Failover**
  - Backup servers not required to be colocated with subscribers
  - Appropriate for up to six sites, with up to a total of 10,000 phones

IP Telephony Infrastructure Design

Ask the following questions when evaluating an infrastructure for IP telephony support:

- What features are required for campus infrastructure devices (for example, inline power)?
- Does the existing cable plant require upgrading (for example, upgrading Cat 3 to Cat 5)?

- What Enterprise Edge features are required (for example, QoS features)?
- Is extra bandwidth required for the WAN?
- Is extras bandwidth required for the LAN?

When provisioning bandwidth, do not exceed 75 percent of a link speed. Use the following formula to calculate required bandwidth for voice traffic:

Voice Bearer Traffic (bps) = (Packet Payload + Header Size in bits) * (Packet Rate per Second)

Because of voice's latency-sensitive nature, quality of service is especially important for IP telephony networks. Building access switches can place different traffic types into different queues, as can the building distribution switch. The building distribution switch can also perform classification. A router connecting to the WAN can also limit bandwidth using traffic shaping or link efficiency mechanisms (for example, link fragmentation and interleaving and compression) to optimize low bandwidth WAN links.

Traffic engineering techniques determine how much bandwidth is required to support voice demands during peak usage times. The goal is to prevent anyone from ever receiving a busy signal. As a designer, you must select an appropriate grade of service (GoS), which determines the percentage of denied call attempts during peak times. A typical GoS is 1 percent.

When creating dial plans, your goal is to make the new IP telephony system as transparent to your end users as possible. Therefore, attempt to maintain extension numbers for users. If you are combining multiple sites that have overlapping ranges of extension numbers, you might have to define "digit transformations," where your users enter a "site code" before they enter the actual extension number.

Management, Availability, Security, and QoS Considerations

IP telephony networks can leverage the Cisco CallManager and CiscoWorks GUI interfaces to aid in managing voice networks. CiscoWorks VoIP Health Monitor (VHM) monitors the status, reachability, and environmental conditions of infrastructure hardware. VHM can also simulate an IP phone call to proactively test various transactions.

As in the campus infrastructure, high availability is a major design consideration for VoIP networks. For example, VoIP gateways must re-home to another CallManager in the event of a CallManager failure.

Similarly, in a centralized call-processing model, IP phones at a remote site must make calls even if the WAN link to the central site fails. Survivable Remote Site Telephony (SRST) makes this possible by allowing an H.323 IOS gateway to use its call forwarding intelligence in the absence of a CallManager.

When securing a VoIP network, use the same best practices presented previously for the campus infrastructure. Also, separate the voice traffic from the data traffic by placing the voice traffic in an "auxiliary VLAN." A Cisco IP phone can place voice and data packets into different VLANs.

Content Networking

Components of Content Networking

Content networking allows content (such as web pages) to be stored at strategic geographic locations in the network in order to provide content to the end user while minimizing the burden on WAN bandwidth. The Cisco content networking solution has five components:

- **Content caching**—Caches content from servers to provide content to end users
- **Content switching**—Load balances requests across content engines (that is, network appliances that are responsible for locally storing content on internal hard drives) or servers that contain the content
- **Content routing**—Directs users to the appropriate content resource
- **Content distribution and management**—Intelligently distributes content to geographically dispersed content servers
- **Services**—Leverages AVVID components, such as high availability, QoS, and security in the context of content networking.

You can perform caching at multiple network locations. For example, the end user might leverage *application and browser caches* to serve up content from the user's local hard drive. *Proxy and transparent caches* are often used at the edge of a WAN to serve up as much content as possible to local users, without having to retrieve content over the WAN. Finally, *reverse proxy servers* are often located in a server farm to offload content from servers and provide content in response to a user request.

Content Caching

Transparent caching dynamically intercepts requests directed outside of the network and redirects those requests to a local content engine. However, proxy caching requires that a user's application (for example, a browser) point directly to the content engine.

Transparent Caching

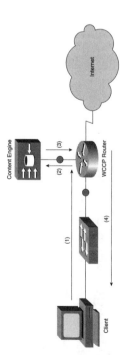

1 A client sends a request for a web page.

2 The WCCP router intercepts the web request and redirects the request to a local content engine.

3 The content engine sends the requested web content to the WCCP router.

4 The WCCP router returns the web content to the client.

A reverse proxy content engine is located close to a server, and the content engine proactively offloads static content from the server. The content engine can service those requests when requests come into the server.

Content Switching

Content-switching load balances multiple requests across multiple content engines or servers. Policy-based redirection can also be specified. As another benefit, content switching enhances denial of service (DoS) protection.

Content Routing

Content routing is an automated approach to determining the "best" location from which to retrieve specific content. A content router can be implemented in one of two ways:

- **Direct mode**—A user sends out a DNS request, and that request is forwarded to a local content router. The content router forwards the DNS request to multiple content routing agents at different locations, and the first content routing agent to respond is deemed at the "best" site. The user's DNS request is resolved to the IP address of the "best" site.

- **WCCP mode**—The web Cache Communication Protocol (WCCP) allows a router to determine whether a request should be sent directly to the destination, or if it should be redirected to a content engine. If the content engine does not have the requested content, the content engine retrieves the content and makes it available for future requests.

Content Distribution and Management

Cisco Content Distribution Manager (CDM) is a web-based utility that can intelligently push content to multiple content engines. The CDM uses self-organizing distributed architecture (SODA) to keep track of which content is located on which content engine.

Services

Content network increases the availability of network resources by making content more readily accessible. However, continue to leverage the other intelligent network services specified in the AVVID framework, including security, IP multicast, and QoS. Proper deployment of these services makes content networking even more efficient in delivering content to clients.

Designing Content Networks

- **Topology**—Place content networking devices in appropriate locations. For example, verify that content networking does not force traffic down a suboptimal path.

- **Redundancy**—Use high availability features, such as HSRP, to ensure content networking devices are accessible. Also, verify that load balancing is performed across devices located at a single site.

- **Capacity**—Ensure that a cache's storage space is sufficient to yield significant bandwidth savings. Specifically, a content engine requires enough storage space to accommodate 24 to 72 hours-worth of requests. Also, select a content engine that is capable of supporting peak usage times.

- Caching—Use appropriate caching approaches for various locations. For example, reverse proxy caching is appropriate for server farms, while transparent caching is appropriate for routers in the campus or the remote edge. If used at all, the legacy proxy caching approach is most appropriate at the egress point of the remote edge network.

Designing Content Networking Solutions

Consider a *web caching* design. Strategically place content engines at locations that prevent unnecessary WAN access. For example, remote offices and leverage content switching for server farms capable of mirroring information are often appropriate locations for content engines.

Next, consider an *e-commerce* content networking design. Scale content networking devices to provide high availability and to minimize response times. Because e-commerce transactions deal with sensitive information, appropriate security measures are a critical part of your design.

Finally, consider a *streaming media* content networking solution. Streaming media is often a good candidate for the Cisco Content Distribution Manager (CDM), where content (for example, a video announcement from the CEO to the employees) can be intelligently pushed out to geographically dispersed content engines. When the CDM receives a client request for the streaming content, the client is redirected to the appropriate content engine.

Storage Networking

Need for Storage Networking

Traditionally, when network administrators needed additional storage, they either added hard drives to servers or added servers. However, another approach, made possible with the advent of storage networking, is to consolidate storage on dedicated storage appliances.

Two primary approaches to storage networking are storage area networks (SANs) and Network Attached Storage (NAS) devices. Consider the distinctions between these options:

- SAN—A SAN is an independent network that is specifically designed for interconnecting storage devices. Most SANs use Fibre Channel connections and require a media converter to connect to an IP network. SANs are appropriate for high-volume, write-intensive applications, such as a database application.

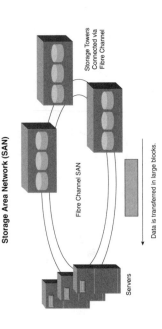

Storage Area Network (SAN)

Storage Towers Connected via Fibre Channel

Fibre Channel SAN

Servers

Data is transferred in large blocks.

- NAS—NAS devices allow file storage over an IP network. The NAS device might appear as a UNIX NFS volume, for example. NAS is appropriate for file sharing applications.

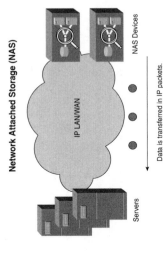

Network Attached Storage (NAS)

NAS Devices

IP LAN/WAN

Servers

Data is transferred in IP packets.

Network Storage Models

With a SAN, multiple disk towers can interconnect using SCSI and Fibre Channel protocols. This approach allows data to be transferred in large blocks without breaking it up, as with a LAN. Therefore, with a SAN, your applications receive very fast access to large volumes of data.

A NAS device is essentially a network file server and can thus work with NFS file systems for UNIX or the Common Internet File System (CIFS) in a Windows environment. Therefore, NAS is often used for file sharing, e-mail services, and web services. While both SANs and NAS devices provide access to file resources, visualize the SAN being its own network and not impacting LAN traffic.

Underlying Technology

Very high-speed technologies are required to support the massive storage that SANs and NAS devices provide. Here are some examples of these technologies:

- **Fibre Channel**—Fibre Channel technologies typically support transfer rates of 100 Mbps or greater. Fibre Channel over IP (FCIP) allows you to interconnect SAN islands over an IP network by encapsulating Fibre Channel communication in IP packets.

- **iSCSI**—The Internet Small Computer System Interface (iSCSI) encapsulates SCSI data and command frames into IP packets. Cisco has iSCSI routers that connect a Fibre Channel fabric to an IP network. iSCSI can span the WAN, and applications that can tolerate delay can use iSCSI as a backup transport to a remote site's storage devices.

Storage Network Services

As you design your storage networks, consider how to manage devices remotely. Also, because storage networks typically service mission-critical data, identify high availability features for the storage network.

To secure storage network transactions, consider isolating storage in a separate VLAN and using access control lists (ACLs) to limit access to storage resources. RADIUS or TACACS+ can be used to authenticate iSCSI connections, and IPSec can encrypt FCIP traffic as it tunnels across the network.

Leverage QoS tools to give priority treatment to iSCSI traffic. Also, limiting the bandwidth usage by other traffic can protect FCIP.

A storage network's bandwidth demands can often be accommodated using EtherChannel, which logically bundles multiple physical connections. For example, on a Catalyst 6500 series switch, you could bundle eight 1 Gbps connections into a single EtherChannel. If those links run in full duplex mode, the theoretical throughput approaches 16 Gbps. FastEthernet (that is, 100 Mbps Ethernet) can still be used for applications with lower bandwidth requirements.

Designing Storage Networks

Ask the following questions when designing a storage network:

- Do applications require backup capabilities or realtime access?
- What are the traffic patterns for each application?
- How much bandwidth is required for each application?
- What special needs do applications have for availability, security, and quality of service?

When designing your storage network, you can allow clients to access the storage resource in different ways. For example, you can use an iSCSI connection to send SCSI command and data over an IP network.

In addition to storage over the LAN, you can also conduct storage over the WAN or MAN. For example, perhaps you wish to perform a backup to an off-site location, or you might want several locations to consolidate their storage to support applications such as data mining. Because these remote sites connect via an IP-based WAN or MAN, you can use storage technologies such as iSCSI or FCIP, provided that sufficient bandwidth is available.

Notes

Notes

Notes

Notes

Notes

Notes

Notes

Notes

Notes

Notes

Notes

Notes

Notes

Notes

Notes